POWER WORDS

Devotional Studies for Youth Bible Study Leaders

Edited by Thomas A. Nummela

Consultants

Jennifer AlLee, Steve Christopher, Tom Doyle, Roger Howard, Joan Lilley, Jay Reed, Tom Rogers, Carolyn Sims, and Roger Sonnenberg

Contributors

Steve Christopher, Roger Howard, Joan Lilley, Jay Reed, Carolyn Sims, and Roger Sonnenberg

Cover design by Mark Bernard

Cindi Anderson, assistant to the editor

Your comments and suggestions concerning the material are appreciated. Please write to Editor, Youth Bible Studies, Concordia Publishing House, 3558 S. Jefferson Avenue, St. Louis, MO 63118-3968.

Scripture quotations are taken from the HOLY BIBLE, NEW INTERNATIONAL VERSION®. NIV®. Copyright © 1973, 1978, 1984 by International Bible Society. Used by permission of Zondervan Publishing House. All rights reserved.

Copyright © 1995 Concordia Publishing House
3558 South Jefferson Avenue, St. Louis, MO 63118-3968
Manufactured in the United States of America

All rights reserved. No part of this publication may be reproduced, stored in a retrieval system, or transmitted, in any form or by any means, electronic, mechanical, photocopying, recording, or otherwise, without the prior written permission of Concordia Publishing House.

1   2   3   4   5   6   7   8   9   10   04   03   02   01   00   99   98   97   96   95

About Power Words and Power Plays

You are holding a set of 24 personal devotional studies that focus on some of the most powerful texts of Scripture. These studies were written to help Bible study leaders and others understand and teach others how the power of God's Word works in their daily lives—what we frequently call sanctification.

Each devotion includes questions for reflection and resources for additional study. You may use these devotions for personal or group study. Consider connecting with other Bible study leaders and youth leaders in your congregation or community for regular study and personal sharing.

These studies follow the arrangement and scriptural texts of *Power Plays*—two books of skit-supported youth Bible studies. *Power Plays* applies these Bible passages and the power of God's Word to corresponding areas in the lives of young people. The two units in this book correspond to *Power Plays, Book 1* and *Power Plays, Book 2* (CPH 1995, order numbers 20-2627 and 20-2628). This allows *Power Words* to be used also as in-depth preparation for the youth Bible study leader who uses the *Power Play* studies. The brief skits included in these studies and the significant issues they address give them strong appeal for high-school-age youth.

Introduction

God provides power in the lives of His people. His power works our salvation as Paul says in Romans 1:16, "I am not ashamed of the gospel, because it is the power of God for the salvation of everyone who believes: first for the Jew, then for the Gentile." God also provides the continuing power of our new life of faith. "I have been crucified with Christ and I no longer live, but Christ lives in me. The life I live in the body, I live by faith in the Son of God, who loved me and gave Himself for me" (Galatians 2:20).

This power for daily living, our sanctification, is frequently misunderstood or underestimated. Many clearly and correctly ascribe their salvation to God's action alone but credit their growth in discipleship, or lack thereof, to their own efforts—in misplaced pride or despair.

The power of Christ at work in us through the Holy Spirit enables us to grow in faith and in good works, which are the evidence of faith (James 2:18). There is nurturing power in the Gospel, the good news of forgiveness through the suffering and death of Christ. We receive that power as we hear God's Word and share in the Sacraments He has provided. The Gospel frees us from the guilt and enslavement of past sin. Each day it offers us new strength to live according to God's will. The Gospel is that kind of power.

This book explores 24 issues in life. As we see God's forgiveness and grace in each situation, God empowers us to reject sin and grow in lives of discipleship. In each issue we see God's powerful Word at work.

God will be at work in your study of these "power Words." His grace will supply new life just as He promises. ✝

Contents

Unit One

1.	**Immanuel in a World of Doubt** (*Power Plays, Book 1, Study 1*—"There's a God? So What!")	6
2.	**Certainty of Salvation** (*Power Plays, Book 1, Study 2*—"God's Sure Plan of Salvation")	9
3.	**Just Who Do You Think You Are?** (*Power Plays, Book 1, Study 3*—"I Wish I Could Control Myself")	11
4.	**Be a Somebody, Not a Nobody** (*Power Plays, Book 1, Study 4*—"How Do I Look to God?")	14
5.	**Freedom from Guilt** (*Power Plays, Book 1, Study 5*—"Guilty! Now What?")	16
6.	**Parents, Rights, and Responsibilities** (*Power Plays, Book 1, Study 6*—"I Have Rights Too!")	18
7.	**Home Is Where the Hassle Is** (*Power Plays, Book 1, Study 7*—"When My Family Fights")	20
8.	**Everlasting Love in a Divorced Society** (*Power Plays, Book 1, Study 8*—"Staying Whole, Even if Your Parents Split")	22
9.	**What Does God Want from Me?** (*Power Plays, Book 1, Study 9*—"What Now, God?")	24
10.	**Simple People with an Awesome Message** (*Power Plays, Book 1, Study 10*—"Good News for Your Friends")	26
11.	**The King and I** (*Power Plays, Book 1, Study 11*—"What Comes First?")	28
12.	**Satan, Lord of Darkness** (*Power Plays, Book 1, Study 12*—"The Dark Side")	30

Unit Two

1. Love Me, Love My Problems? (*Power Plays, Book 2, Study 1*— "I Can Help!")	32
2. Popularity (*Power Plays, Book 2, Study 2*— "The Price of Popularity")	35
3. Divided Loyalties between Friends (*Power Plays, Book 2, Study 3*— "When Friends Make Me Choose")	37
4. Career Decisions (*Power Plays, Book 2, Study 4*— "What Will I Do with My Life?")	40
5. The Honor Roll (*Power Plays, Book 2, Study 5*— "How Will I Know When I've Got It Made?")	42
6. In Sexuality—a Pig or a Bride? (*Power Plays, Book 2, Study 6*— "Special People, Special Purpose")	45
7. The Value of a Life (*Power Plays Book 2, Study 7*— "Who Values Life?")	48
8. Positive Sexuality (*Power Plays, Book 2, Study 8*— "God Created Sex!")	50
9. When Is Enough? (*Power Plays, Book 2, Study 9*— "Me First?")	52
10. Music and Its Influence (*Power Plays, Book 2, Study 10*— "My Music—To God's Glory!")	55
11. Heroes (*Power Plays, Book 2, Study 11*— "Whom Do You Admire Most and Why?")	58
12. Our Violent God? (*Power Plays, Book 2, Study 12*— "Peace of Mind in Violent Times")	60

UNIT 1

See Power Plays, Book 1, Study 1—

"There's a God? So What!"

Immanuel in a World of Doubt

An uneasy tension pulls on us in those "uncomfortable" places—a downtown street, the back of the bus, or a local park. Ordinarily these places are fine. But at times they are uncomfortable places because of people—street people. Largely ignored and cast off, such people are a segment of a society with diminishing hope. They unsettle us because we have a God of hope, a God who says, "Leave your orphans; I will protect their lives. Your widows too can trust in me" (Jer. 49:11). We are troubled and ask, "Where is God in this? Where is the God of hope for these people?"

That same question arises as we watch news reports of war-torn countries, starving children, and natural disasters that claim hundreds of lives. We hear the message of Scripture, "God is peace; God cares," yet in the streets we see escalating hatred and violence. Is God absent from the world and the people He has made?

Parallel thoughts may have troubled the people in the region of the Gerasenes during the time of Christ. They were made uncomfortable by a kind of "street person"—demon-possessed and homeless. Mark tells the story in chapter 5 of his gospel. People had tried to help the man, but no one could. People must have passed by wondering, "Where is God in this? Where is the God of peace and care for this raving lunatic, this demon-plagued man? Perhaps this one is just beyond the scope of God's care. Does God care for just some people, but not for all?"

An unbelieving world may respond, "God might be okay for you, but He's not really for me. I mean, look at my life. If God really

> **Bible Text**
> "I pray that out of His glorious riches He may strengthen you with power through His Spirit in your inner being, so that Christ may dwell in your hearts through faith. And I pray that you, being rooted and established in love, may have power, together with all the saints, to grasp how wide and long and high and deep is the love of Christ."
> **(Ephesians 3:16–18)**

> This is a great mystery—the cross, the place where God meets us to say, "I love you."

cares …? Look at the world. If God were really present …," and on it goes. All too often we have no good response. We can only listen. Perhaps those very doubts are our own.

It may help us then to seriously ask those persistent questions: "God if You really are loving, then why … ?" "If You're the strength of my life, Jesus, then how come … ?" Either God is really present and in this world or we are perpetuating a myth. The dilemma confronts us as much today as it did for the people at the time of the Christ.

"When [the people] came to Jesus, they saw the man who had been possessed by the legion of demons, sitting there, dressed and in his right mind …" (Mark 5:15). And the people's response? Mark tells us that the people asked Jesus to leave the region in response to this miracle, angry about the destruction of their pigs. The cured demoniac begged Jesus to take him along. Two totally different responses to the same man, God's Son.

Each side had its own perspective. One sees tremendous blessing as demons are driven into the herd of swine. The other asks, "How could God be in this, destroying our livelihood and animals?" From a pig farmer's point of view, Jesus was a disaster. From that of the ex-demoniac, He was a miracle worker, a healer. Each responded according to his human condition.

Is that not also the problem in our day? When we say, "If God really cares, He would …," we betray our human notion of what we expect His good will to be. We have already determined how God needs to act in order to be good—to please us. When we are confronted with poverty, crime, and sin in the world around us, we have preconceived notions of how a good God should act. How differently Paul prayed for the Ephesians—and us. "I pray that out of His glorious riches He may strengthen you with power through His Spirit in your inner being, so that Christ may dwell in your hearts through faith. And I pray that you, being rooted and established in love, may have power, together with all the saints, to grasp how wide and long and high and deep is the love of Christ" (Eph. 3:16–18).

The people in Jesus' time saw the persecution and the suffering around them, and "knew" how the Messiah should respond. They expected the forceful return to the golden years of the kingdom of David. Yet instead of a mighty warrior, the Messiah was a humble servant. His weapon was not a sword but a cross.

> In a world of so many "whys" we have a huge "because."

For Further Study

"Does God really care?" is a penetrating question for Christians and non-Christians alike, especially in such a broken world. Below are some verses to encourage you about God's presence and His intimate involvement in this world.

Matt. 28:20—Jesus is with us always.

Is. 43—God is with us through the trouble of each day.

Ps. 34:18—God will be close to the brokenhearted.

Rom. 8:38–39—God's love for us is inseparable.

Acts 17:24–28—God's relationship to us is one of love.

1 Cor. 2:6–16—Because of the revelation by the Spirit we can better understand God's mystery.

For Reflection

1. Why are questions about God's presence and involvement in our lives so tough to address? Do they show a lack of faith? ignorance? a hard heart?

2. Consider some of the things in this world that raise doubts or questions about God's ways. How does the truth of "God meeting man at the cross" help with our doubts and questions?

3. What would be your most helpful reaction where others (friends, family members, or students) express doubts about God's presence and love?

This is a great mystery—the cross, the place where God meets us to say, "I love you." His love for us is not measured by the outcome of our situation, on whether or not God acts like we think He's supposed to, for situations change like the tides. Our perceptions and views of the same situation can be as opposite as those of the pig farmers and the delivered demoniac.

Rising above all that is the cross, sure and unchanging proof that God is among His people. It shows us "how wide and long and high and deep is the love of Christ." In all our situations and conditions, we have that promise of God's never-failing, unconditional love for us. In a world of so many "whys" we have a huge "because"—*John 3:16, "For God so loved the world that He gave His one and only Son, that whoever believes in Him shall not perish but have eternal life."*

By the mystery of the cross we can live in the tension of uncomfortable situations with their nagging questions. For as we struggle with those very doubts and situations, we find the strength and power of the Spirit at work in us, "so that Christ may dwell in [our] hearts through faith."

Prayer

The psalmists frequently speak very directly to God, asking about His intentions and requesting His help (see Psalms 10 and 13). Take a moment to list any doubts and questions that you have about God right now. Speak these to God in prayer. Ask Him to help you understand and know Him better that you might see how He is working even in uncomfortable situations.

See Power Plays, Book 1, Study 2—

"God's Sure Plan of Salvation"

Certainty of Salvation

St. Paul was in prison and close to death when he wrote again to Timothy. Even in his suffering and imprisonment, his eyes were focused firmly on the one sure truth, that His God loved Him. He knew that eternal life was his and that, no matter what happened to him or what this life had in store for him, God's arms were wrapped firmly around him. He was certain that salvation was his.

How do we define salvation? One dictionary of theology includes almost two complete pages of explanation, including Bible references and comparative studies. Though the information was very impressive, three words stand out at the very bottom of the second page: "See also *Savior*." No matter how hard we try to define the word, the essential truth still remains, "See also Savior." Sometimes the truth is so simple it seems unbelievable.

A few years ago, a friend of mine introduced me to the man she was about to marry. I noticed that the knees of his otherwise immaculate suit were quite worn out. Observing my gaze he said proudly, "I spend at least two hours a day walking on my knees on the gravel road behind my house as penance, to prove to God that I believe in Him and am worthy of salvation." I was shocked. He was serious.

God's love at Christ's expense

We are not "worthy of salvation"—no one is—but God has promised it to us. Salvation is not something we inherit because of what we have done but because of what He has done. It is God's free gift of love at Christ's expense.

An astute young woman put it this way: "I don't have any trouble believing that God can forgive everyone else. I just don't believe that He can forgive me." But God's grace is a gift. God instantly forgives all those with faith in Him. We carry unnecessary and foolish guilt when we feel downtrodden by sins He has forgiven.

God loves all of His children. We can do nothing to earn salvation. It was purchased and paid for on a cross on Golgotha outside of Jerusalem nearly 2,000 years ago.

Bible Text

"That is why I am suffering as I am. Yet I am not ashamed because I know whom I have believed, and am convinced that He is able to guard what I have entrusted to Him for that Day" **(2 Timothy 1:12).**

For Further Study

The following Bible passages relate to salvation:

Ex. 15:2; Ps. 118:14; Is. 12:2—God is our strength.

Ps. 28:8—God is our fortress.

Is. 33:2—We plea to God for salvation.

2 Cor. 1:5—We have comfort in Christ.

John 5:24—We have assurance of salvation.

Matt. 1:21–23—A prophecy is fulfilled.

Luke 2:25–32—The account of Simeon and Jesus.

Rom. 1:16—We have the Gospel, the power of salvation.

For Reflection

1. Imagine that someone totally unfamiliar with Christianity asked you to explain salvation. What would you say?

2. Think of a time you experienced Christ's forgiveness in your own life. Describe your feelings. Consider how you might share your experience as an example to students or others.

3. We know through God's Word that He forgives us all our sin through the work of Jesus, His Son. But often we don't experience or feel this forgiveness as we should. There are times when it hits us and times when it doesn't. Think about a time Christ's forgiveness really hit home for you. What were your feelings? How did you respond?

Time and time again in the Scriptures, Jesus presents examples of God's complete forgiveness. In the story of the Lost Son (Luke 15:11–24), not only does the father welcome his son home after the son has squandered all of his inheritance, he literally *runs* to meet him. This loving account of a parent for a child helps us to more completely understand God's love.

Those of us who are parents know how angry and frustrated we can become with our children. But, no matter what they do, we never stop loving them. We experience terrible pain when they are hurting, and incredible joy when they are happy. If we, hindered by sin, can show this much love, how much greater is the love of the God who created the universe and set us in it?

God's promise of forgiveness and salvation is the key to our Christianity. It is no surprise then to find it so prevalent in Scripture. In Acts 2:38–39, Peter calls us to repent and be baptized in the name of Christ for the forgiveness of sin and tells us that "the promise is for you and your children and for all who are far off—for all whom the Lord our God will call." John refers to salvation and eternal life 36 times in his Gospel (e.g., John 3:16–17), and 13 times in 1 John ("And this is the testimony: God has *given* us eternal life, and this life is in His Son" 1 John 5:11). The key word here is "given"—not earned, *given*. God's grace *is* free, His love *is* eternal. No matter what we do, we simply cannot outgive our God or cause Him to stop loving us.

R. E. O. White tries to explain salvation this way in *An Evangelical Dictionary of Theology*, (p. 968):

> "Salvation is therefore, first, acquittal, despite just condemnation, on the ground of Christ's expiation of sin (Rom. 3:21–22); and second, deliverance by the invasive power of the Spirit of holiness, the Spirit of the risen Christ. The faith which accepts and assents to Christ's death on our behalf also unites us to Him so closely that with Him we die to sin and rise to new life (Rom. 6:1–2). … By the same process, death is overcome and believers are prepared for life everlasting (6:13, 22–23; 8:11)."

Noted author and lecturer Brennan Manning tells a story about a woman who claimed she was in direct communication with our Lord. Wishing to disparage her authenticity, a bishop of the church told her to ask God what sins he had confessed on a particular day at a particular time. After several days the woman responded. "I asked God what sins you confessed," she said, "and His answer was, 'I don't remember, I just don't remember.' "

The woman's clever response contains an accurate truth. "As far as the east is from the west, so far has He removed our transgressions from us" (Ps. 103:12). "I will forgive their wickedness and will remember their sins no more" (Hebrews 8:12). Through Christ's sacrifice on the cross, our debt is fully paid and our slate fully clean. Salvation is ours, guarded for us by faith in Christ. Thanks be to God!

Prayer

Dear heavenly Father, You have given us so many reminders of Your grace. Help us to see Your love in all that surrounds us, in our relationships with others, and in Your Word. Help us to always remember that Your grace is a free gift to each of us through faith in Christ. Help us to always know that we are Your children and trust in Your love now and for all eternity. We ask this in Jesus' name. Amen.

See Power Plays, Book 1, Study 3—

"I Wish I Could Control Myself"

Just Who Do You Think You Are?

"Hypocrite!" The label burns. Call me weak; call me "only human;" call me "chief of sinners." But hypocrite? Not that!

Hypocrites pretend to be what they are not. They act holy in public, but are holy terrors when no one is watching. They talk big, but act small. They make promises they won't keep. They sit piously in the pew with their spouse on Sunday morning after an earlier 30-minute argument. They teach Sunday school but don't have time for family devotions. They make marriage vows but neglect relationships.

It is an ugly picture, but an all too familiar one. Enough to make most of us feel really guilty.

St. Paul had a lot of experience with hypocrites. As he penned the second chapter of Galatians, he remembers a time when he was particularly upset with Peter—again! Peter, who wanted to walk on water but sank; Peter who boasted, "I will die with you," and then denied any acquaintance; Peter was at it again. He gladly ate with the Gentiles and eloquently proclaimed their equality before God. But when James came for a visit, Peter turned away from his ethnically-embarrassing friends.

Paul was so upset that he confronted Peter on the spot. "Who do you think you are?" he exploded. "You claim to be one of God's elect, but you live like a heathen! Your bad example is causing others to live like heathen too. You know that we are saved by grace alone, yet you act like you're bound by the Law!"

"Hypocrite!"

Bible Text
I have been crucified with Christ and I no longer live, but Christ lives in me **(Galatians 2:20).**

> Paul and Peter, and you and I, all have the same problem. It's called sin.

For Further Study

For a deeper look at this issue of "simultaneously saint and sinner," check the following references.

Saint Paul's frustration — Rom. 7 (especially verses 14–25)

God's No and God's Yes, CPH 1973, by C. F. W. Walther

Paul ought to know a hypocrite when he saw one. He thought one lived in his mirror. The Paul who chastised Peter was the same man who later wrote to the Romans, "For what I do is not the good I want to do; no, the evil I do not want to do—this I keep on doing. … What a wretched man I am!" (Rom. 7:19, 24)

Can you imagine Paul's shame? Everyone thought he was a great apostle. Some folks even called him a god. The Corinthians chose him like a team captain and bragged about him. But Paul didn't feel very godlike. He felt fear and loneliness, pride and doubt, and frustration and guilt.

Paul and Peter, you and I—we all have the same problem. It's called sin. We also have the same answer. It's called grace. These two components are the sum and substance of who we are.

> To Him, you are "saint" — always and forever, saint!

The sin part is obvious. No child needs to be taught to do what is wrong. It just comes naturally. But through Baptism and by God's grace, sinners are made into something entirely different—saints. Not a plastic saint that stands inert and never does anything wrong because it never does anything at all, but an industrial strength saint who cares about people and honors God and is brave and faithful and true—for real.

Peter, the denier, was also Peter the defender; and Paul, "chief of sinners," was at the same time Paul, giant among the apostles. God looks at us through the eyes of Christ and does not see the sin at all. He sees, instead, the perfect life of Jesus and declares us sin-free.

We are not saints because of what we do. We are saints because of who we are. We are God's forgiven people.

Hypocrites pretend to be what they are not. Sinners, like you and me, are not pretending anything. We sin because it is our nature. By God's grace we know it, we confess it, and we combat it. When saints, like you and me, behave like the saints we are, we are not pretending either. It is Christ's nature to be perfect, and He lives in us.

What an amazing thing! Jesus, who is perfect, took on our sinful human nature, and crucified it. The ultimate power of sin over our bodies and souls was destroyed by the death of His body on the cross. Now, Paul says, it is in our very human bodies that we are free to live as God's forgiven sinners, as God's redeemed saints.

Are you plagued by the things you do wrong or fail to do right? God has already forgiven you. Also let Him have the burden of your guilt. Yes, you are a sinner. But you also are the one for whom Jesus died. Is Christ alive in you—giving, caring, and accomplishing things in His Kingdom? Praise God! Acknowledge His power at work in you. You are a saint. That's how God lives in this world.

Do others disappoint you? Do people fail to live up to your expectations? They are sinners. Forgive them as Christ forgives. Do you see God's people in action—doing heroic deeds, demonstrating patience, love, and kindness for God and each other? Thank God! They are saints. Christ is at work in them.

"Just who do you think you are, anyway?" In the light of God's Word, you know who you are—saint/sinner still. By the grace of God, He knows you, He has made you, and He calls you by name. To Him, you are "saint"—always and forever, saint!

Prayer

Pray for Christian friends who are struggling with a particular sin.
Pray for forgiveness for your failures.
Pray for confidence and power to live as a saint in this world.
Pray for those who are suffering because of their faith, that they may be protected and given courage in the face of danger.

For Reflection

1. List some "fallen" heroes—popular public figures who were discredited. Recall some of their "saintly" characteristics. What was your first reaction to their sins?

2. Who looks up to you as a role model? Have you ever knowingly disappointed them? What would you say/do if they discovered you in some sin?

3. Finish these sentences: I feel most like a sinner when …

    I feel most like a saint when …

4. What might you say to people who expect you to be perfect?

5. Have you ever felt like a hypocrite? Why? How will Paul's words in Gal. 2:20 be of encouragement to you when you feel that way in the future? What other passages in Scripture have you found to be helpful in this situation?

See Power Plays, Book 1, Study 4—"How Do I Look to God?".

Be a Somebody, Not a Nobody

Those who study the social sciences note a correlation between positive self-image and positive performance among people of all ages. Those who are self-confident and optimistic about their potential in life achieve more than those who see themselves negatively and are filled with doubt. Since this is true, those who know God and live in faith have a unique advantage in the world, for our positive self-concept is rooted in the certain love of God, shown to us especially by the gift of His Son. The world tries to arrive at a positive self-concept by finding it within themselves. This leads to a denial of guilt, to depression, or to a self-righteous attitude. The Christian, on the other hand, sees the person God has made him or her to be in Christ—a son or daughter of God Himself. Paul lays a foundation for our positive self-concept in Eph. 1:3–6.

First, he praises God for our every spiritual blessing. He reminds us that there is nothing held back—God gives us everything. Not only do we receive it in the heavenly realms, but also here on earth. True, these blessings are veiled by sin on this side of heaven, but they are given nonetheless. Some may think that positive identity can be found only in some personal merit for God's blessings, that we can feel good about ourselves only if we have earned the good things in life. Scripture reminds us that, even when there is *no* obvious reason for God's choice, we can rejoice that God has blessed us anyway.

Paul reminds us that we were chosen by God to be holy and blameless before the world was even created! Just as He loved His own Son, Jesus, before the world was created (John 17:24), so He chose to love us before all time began. Who doesn't identify with the short, non-athletic kid who is always last to be chosen when captains picked their team members. Even those who do not seem

Bible Text

Praise be to the God and Father of our Lord Jesus Christ, who has blessed us in the heavenly realms with every spiritual blessing in Christ. For He chose us in Him before the creation of the world to be holy and blameless in His sight. In love He predestined us to be adopted as His sons through Jesus Christ, in accordance with His pleasure and will—to the praise of His glorious grace, which He has freely given us in the One He loves **(Ephesians 1:3–6).**

God declares us to be holy and blameless.

to have many skills or talents can take great comfort in the fact that God Himself has chosen them.

God declares us to be holy and blameless. Our first reaction may be one of guilt, since we cannot become holy and blameless ... on our own. However, the very definition of the word—*holy* means "set apart"—leads us to the source of righteousness.

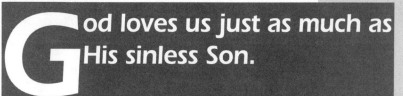

Just as Moses was set apart from his people by God to lead them out of Egypt, so God sets us apart to be blameless. Just as Moses protested that he was not worthy of the task, so we despair that we cannot measure up to God's standard of being blameless. Just as God gave Moses the resources he needed, so He gives us the righteousness of Christ. Jesus, the perfect, blameless Son of God, takes the blame for us. "For the sheep the Lamb has bled, sinless in the sinners stead."

Paul describes us as adopted sons of God. The term *son* designates us to be heirs to the family fortune—salvation and all its blessings. Some who have been adopted may feel poorly about themselves because they may focus on being unwanted by their birth parents. It is equally true, however, that their adoptive parents wanted them above all other possible choices. This can forge a strong self-image. On a more personal level, God adopts us, despite all our weaknesses and sin, and loves us just as much as His sinless Son. Sons in Bible times, especially those born first, enjoyed most-favored status of all children; as Christians, we share in Jesus' status as first-born, only, righteous Son through our adoption, and it is "according to His pleasure and will." God wants us, and He is happy with us!

Finally, Paul explains the reason for God's choice. God adopts us as His most-favored children **to the praise of His glorious grace.** The result of His grace in our lives is that His glory will be shown to all who look at us. His free gift in Jesus will ultimately glorify God through all eternity, even as it unites Him with the people He loves.

Whether we call it "self-image," "self-esteem," or even "Christ-esteem," we can be confident that God sees us as His chosen people, set apart to receive the blessings of Jesus Christ and give Him all the glory that is due Him. We *are* somebody; we are His!

Prayer

Dear Lord, thank You for making me a somebody. Help me to share You with all who feel like nobodies, that they may know You as I do, and all of us can praise You. Amen.

For Further Study

God holds you in high esteem. Explore the dimensions of His love in these passages:

Rom. 8:1
Eph. 4:21–24
Eph. 5:25–27
Col. 1:22
1 Peter 1:15–16
1 Peter 2:9–10

For a more extended study of this topic, consider the course **God-Esteem** (part of the Connections Series, CPH © 1994, 20-2472, $3.99 per copy, includes leaders guide), or read **Christ Esteem**, by Don Matzat (Harvest House, 1990).

For Reflection

1. What is implied in each of these terms—self-concept, self-esteem, Christ-esteem? Which do you prefer to use? Why?
2. Of what significance is it that God **chose** us to be His?
3. When someone you know feels unwanted or treated as a nobody, how can you communicate God's love in Jesus to him or her? List one or two specific ways you can do this. Plan to put them into practice.

5

See Power Plays, Book 1, Study 5—

"Guilty! Now What?"

Freedom from Guilt

At times, King David was consumed by guilt. He writes, "When I kept silent, my bones wasted away through my groaning all day long. For day and night your hand was heavy upon me; my strength was sapped as in the heat of summer" (Ps. 32:3–4). What a powerful description of guilt's effect—an oppressive weight that saps strength.

David here reveals the guilt he feels as a result of sin. We experience guilt from a number of directions: guilt for what we do or don't do; guilt even for things we have no control over and have nothing to do with. If there's one thing in abundance in our world today, it's guilt. Endless pointing fingers seem to condemn us for our every thought, word, and deed. At times we see no escape.

Guilt is necessary. It makes us aware of our sinfulness and brokenness. It shows us our need for forgiveness. It is a first step in the process that by God's grace leads us to repentance. But what will keep guilt from crushing us while it does the necessary work?

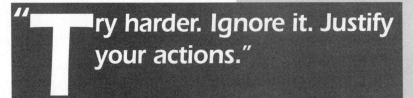

"Try harder. Ignore it. Justify your actions."

John offers a powerful insight in 1 John 4. He talks about the false prophets, claiming God's name, who preach a counterfeit message. Those same false prophets are among us today.

They provide varied and false solutions to guilt. Try harder. Ignore it. Justify your actions. Our society has legalized acts which God has declared abhorrent. People find legal loopholes for atrocious crimes. This sort of daily denial of guilt may affect our lives as God's people. We justify our actions by comparing them with those around us. We look around and see many who are worse—more

Bible Text

You, dear children, are from God and have overcome [the false prophets], because the one who is in you is greater than the one who is in the world **(1 John 4:4).**

sinful than we. Though we may feel better, our guilt remains. All sin, including our acts and lives of unrighteousness, stands condemned before a holy and just God.

Our enemy, "the one who is in the world" seeks to convince us that our guilt can be removed by something—anything—other than Jesus Christ. "If it's legal, it must be okay. Everybody's doing it. You just need to try harder." Or it drives us to despair, "Forget it, you can never be forgiven for that." In the face of this constant barrage, we can lose sight of the truth.

But John has great news. He reminds us that we are God's. We are His chosen, forgiven people. We need not be overwhelmed by our real guilt from sinning against God and the guilt heaped on us by the accusers of this world. "The one who is in [us] is greater than the one who is in the world." Jesus Christ forgives our sin, saves our wounded spirit, and relieves our guilt.

On the cross Jesus won for you a permanent condition—guiltlessness. It's called "righteousness" (2 Cor. 5:21). It means standing before God with no guilt. It is as if Jesus has covered you in a pure white robe—*His* righteousness. It is the free gift of God, given by the Spirit and daily renewed by Him through Word and Sacrament.

God's Word reminds us that guilt is overcome by the forgiving power of the "one who is in you," Jesus Christ. So, as you are struggling with guilt from accusers around you or from your convictions within, draw strength from the One who has forgiven all your sins and is able and eager to keep you pure to the end—Jesus Christ. As we in faith confess our sins, we also hear His words of forgiveness, "Go in peace, your sins are forgiven."

Prayer

Make a list of things for which you feel guilty in your life right now. Over the list, write the words to one of the passages noted above. In prayer, confess your sin to God. Then read aloud the verse you have chosen. Thank God for the assurance of your forgiveness through Jesus Christ.

For Further Study

In a world that would keep us in chains of guilt, Jesus has set us free. Study the following verses for help in your struggle with guilt. Memorize one or more of them as a ready response in helping others.

Rom. 8:1–2—There is no condemnation. We are set free.

John 8:36—The Son sets you free.

2 Cor. 5:21—In Christ we are righteous.

1 John 1:7–9—Jesus cleanses us from all sin.

For Reflection

1. What's the difference between **being** guilty and **feeling** guilty? Which is harder to deal with?
2. Name some ways we try to cover up our guilt. Why do we try so hard to justify or deny it?
3. Think about your family, friends, or co-workers. Who stands out in your mind as needing to hear God's Word of forgiveness? How will you share that Word?

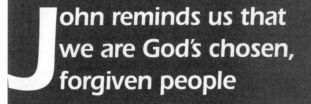

John reminds us that we are God's chosen, forgiven people

See Power Plays, Book 1, Study 6— "I Have Rights Too!"

Parents, Rights, and Responsibilities

A woman in Albuquerque stops at McDonald's to get a quick cup of coffee. She accidently spills the coffee in her lap. She sues McDonald's for making the coffee too hot and wins $650,000.

A couple is making love on a subway track in New York City. They are hit by the train and sue the New York City Transit Authority for injuries sustained.

A commercial on television features a lawyer who looks you in the eye and says, "If you've been hurt in an accident, even if it was your fault, you have some rights. I've defended many accident victims and gotten them millions of dollars. I can help you. Call me today at 1-800-SUE-THEM."

It's an *Adam and Eve* approach to sin. "It was her fault!" Adam suggested. "No, it was really the serpent's fault," exclaimed Eve. We excuse our sin by blaming others. This is true for families as well as individuals. Parents and their children get into the destructive cycle of always blaming others or circumstances for their faults and not taking responsibility.

Johnny comes home with a note from the teacher. The note tells of some misbehavior on the part of Johnny and reports several hours of detention for him after school. Instead of supporting the teacher, the parent rushes to the school principal's office and goes into a rampage, making all sorts of excuses why Johnny can't be blamed for his misbehavior and demanding that the detention be dropped.

A teenager asserts her freedom from the tyranny of parents who demand she be home by 1 a.m. every night.

A father falls in love with a co-worker. He files for divorce, reasoning that for years he's supported his family without even a thank you. Now it's time for him to have some fun in life.

Everyone wants their rights. Nobody seems to want responsibility.

The supreme example of surrendering rights and accepting responsibility was our Lord Jesus Christ. He gave up His rights—even His

Bible Text

Your attitude should be the same as that of Christ Jesus: who, being in very nature God, did not consider equality with God something to be grasped, but made Himself nothing, taking the very nature of a servant, being made in human likeness. And being found in appearance as a man, He humbled Himself and became obedient to death—even death on a cross! **(Philippians. 2:5–8).**

throne in heaven—in order to carry out a God-given responsibility—the redemption of the human race. Though Jesus was truly both God and man, St. Paul tells that He set aside His own glory as God and became as a slave, taking on our humanity, in order to make us His own sons and daughters (Phil. 2:7–8). He was God's servant, submissive to the will of His Father.

We sin, endlessly making excuses why. We are not and cannot be right in and by ourselves. But as a result of Jesus' obedience to the will of His Father, we were made right. Through His life, death, and resurrection we have forgiveness. We are made righteous!

Also, through His obedience to the will of His Father, He was given a "name that is above every name … Lord" (Phil. 2:9, 11a). Isaiah had prophesied that someday everyone everywhere would worship and serve Jesus as Lord (Is. 45:23). Everyone will confess "Jesus Christ is Lord." This simple statement became one of the earliest creeds of the primitive church. (See Rom. 10:9; 1 Cor. 12:3.)

We cannot have a healthy relationship with God unless we recognize our sin and our need for forgiveness. If we were all spiritually healthy—never responsible for any of our mistakes, indiscretions, or by whatever name a person might call his or her sin—Jesus would not have had to come to earth. Yet Jesus was "obedient to death—even death on a cross" in order to keep us from eternal death (Phil. 2:8). We no longer have to make excuses for our sins. We can be honest and say, "I've sinned. Forgive me!" And He forgives and restores us.

Families can regain spiritual health too as they acknowledge their mistakes and accept responsibility for their part in what happens. "I'm sorry, forgive me!" spoken in Christian homes can result in forgiveness because of Jesus Christ. Jesus emptied Himself in order to fill us up with His forgiveness and love. He is a reservoir of forgiveness for us and our families.

Prayer

Adoration. Give praise to God as described in Philippians 2:10–11: " … that at the name of Jesus every knee should bow, in heaven and on earth and under the earth, and every tongue confess that Jesus Christ is Lord, to the glory of God the Father."

Confession. Confess yours sins. Be specific. Avoid excuses. Take responsibility for the sins you committed in thought, word, and deed this last week.

Thanksgiving. Give thanks to God for the fact that He "humbled Himself and became obedient to death—even death on a cross" in order to win for you forgiveness and eternal life (Phil. 2:8).

Supplication. Pray for other family members that they might take responsibility for their actions by God's grace and seek forgiveness.

For Further Study

Study all of Philippians 2. One of the obvious problems in Philippi was the lack of unity among believers. How is any unity affected either positively or negatively by humility? Why were Timothy and Epaphroditus such good examples of how Christian unity should look?

For Reflection

1. Alexander Hamilton described the fall of Athens in this way: "When the freedom they wished for most was freedom from responsibility, then Athens ceased to be free." Are we approaching a similar condition? What could turn the tide? How can your church take a more important role in teaching people responsibility?

2. Martin Luther wrote, "I believe that Jesus Christ, true God, begotten of the Father from eternity, and also true man, born of the Virgin Mary, is my Lord." What does it mean to say, "He's Lord of my life"? When isn't He Lord of your life?

3. What specific things do you need to change to be more like Christ? How do you think others would react to this new you?

4. How will things change as the attitude of Christ described in Phil. 2:5–11 grows in families?

See Power Plays, Book 1, Study 7—

"When My Family Fights"

Home Is Where the Hassle Is

It is hard to find a "traditional" family in today's culture. Few children these days are raised by two parents in their first and only marriage. Some families include only one parent. Some have a variety of "step" parents and siblings. Some consist of grandchildren being raised by their grandparents. Some family groups consist of people not related in any way. However families are configured, all are alike in at least one way. Every family is made up of sinners. No family is free from the consequences and the day-to-day hassles of sin.

Paul addresses this problem in Eph. 4:32. He describes a model for Christian relationships by pleading that we be "kind and compassionate to one another." What a great idea! Imagine what a family would be like if parents and children, husbands and wives, brothers and sisters daily demonstrated such virtues. The trouble is, it will never happen—not without the rest of the story: "… forgiving each other," Paul goes on, "just as in Christ God forgave you." Sometimes family conflicts begin because people are afraid to admit mistakes. They think being wrong will diminish their value. We know we are already perfect in the eyes of God because of Christ's forgiveness. We need not fear imperfection. Forgiven, we can forgive and accept others and their imperfections.

Conflict in families can result from failure to observe the Fourth Commandment. Here God gives us one of the fundamental building blocks of the family—"Honor your father and mother, so that you may live long in the land the LORD your God is giving you" (Ex. 20:12). In the context of Christian love, such honor is not distasteful, but yields God's rich blessing.

Family conflicts also occur because of faulty expectations. Parents expect their children to get good grades, show respect, be honest, and obey. Children expect to have fun, make their own decisions, and have their own way. Husbands expect wives to care for them,

Bible Text

Be kind and compassionate to one another, forgiving each other, just as in Christ God forgave you **(Ephesians 4:32).**

> **Every family is made up of sinners.**

be available to meet their needs, and submit to them in love even when differences occur—to see things the *right* way, *their* way. Wives expect their husbands to care for them, be available to meet their needs, and submit to them in love even when differences occur—to see things the *right* way, *their* way.

When other family members don't live up to our expectations, our instinct is to become angry, to try to make them do things right! Forgive? Sure—*when* they have shaped up.

But the forgiveness Paul talks about is NOT only for the deserving nor is it given only on certain terms. Paul says to forgive "as in Christ God forgave you." God's forgiveness in Christ is unconditional. "While we were yet sinners," Paul says in Romans 5:8, "Christ died for us." Accepting us for who we were, before we ever said we were sorry—while we were sinners and enemies of God—Christ put an end to the conflict between us by demonstrating His love on the cross.

Conflicts cannot be ignored. They will not go away. They must be forgiven. Paul tells us it is possible *even then* to be kind and compassionate, even to a rebellious child or a self-centered spouse. How? By living in the forgiveness God extends *to us* through Christ and extending it to others.

When we are accepted as we are, we need not pretend to be better than we are. A child who can make mistakes and still experience loving care doesn't have as much need to tattle on her sister to make herself look good. A parent who is confident of being forgiven is free to admit being wrong. There is less need to assert authority through force. There is room for give and take in dealing with each other because all members of the family share a common condition.

Dealing with family struggles prepares children to deal with later issues in life. Working through problems constructively with a parent or sibling, praying together for God's guidance and then depending upon it, experiencing the healing that comes after a hurt—we learn these things through conflict as God makes good on His promise to work all things together for good to those who love Him (Rom. 8:28).

God can make your family not conflict-free but conflict-*proof*. Just as a raincoat doesn't keep the rain from falling but protects the wearer from getting wet, so Jesus wraps your family in His protecting arms. Where conflict exists in any part of His family, Jesus is present, healing the hurt, generating the compassion, forgiving the sin. Look to Him for power—and for peace.

Prayer

Pray for spiritual and physical protection for your family.

Ask God to make clear how you can be of particular help to them.

Pray for wisdom to deal with the family situations you face.

Pray for peace in midst of conflicts that arise.

Pray for a good night's sleep when you are worried about those you love, commending them all into God's unfailing care.

For Further Study

Prov. 25:1; 29:11, 22; and 30:33—Solomon speaks about the folly of conflict.

Matt. 5:21–24—Jesus preaches against anger.

James 1:19–26—James describes the believers' behavior.

In each case, the Law is spoken clearly. We know the Law's fulfillment is found in Jesus Christ as God's gift. (See James 1:17.)

For Reflection

1. Do you know someone who is especially difficult to love or forgive? What makes it so difficult? What quality can you find in him/her that you admire? Let that person know.

2. What quality do you see in yourself that others find irritating?

3. Do all issues over which family members disagree have a "right" side and a "wrong" side? Roleplay, discuss, or think through a situation in your family in which you play the part of your child or spouse and he/she plays your part.

See Power Plays, Book 1, Study 8—

"Staying Whole, Even if Your Parents Split"

Everlasting Love in a Divorced Society

Have you ever had your guts ripped out? Well, not literally (because you probably wouldn't be reading this) but figuratively. You know, like getting a test back with a big, red C–, when you thought you did well on it. Or witnessing a fatal car accident where the victim is a small child. Or discovering that a loved one has cancer. Or hearing the words, "I want a divorce."

You know the feeling—an initial shock to your whole system, followed by a numbing sensation. Everything around you kind of moves in surrealistic slow motion. Nothing seems to have any order or make sense. Time stands still. You are alone.

The Scriptures are full of people *getting their guts ripped out:* Job experienced the loss of his family and worldly goods (Job 3:25–26). David wept over Absalom (2 Sam. 18). Jeremiah pleaded with wayward Israel (Jer. 14:17–18). Jesus wept for Jerusalem (Matt. 23:37). God mourns over us. God mourns over us? That's kind of hard to imagine—the God of the universe in anguish and despair.

Yet His cry in Malachi 2:16 is just that. "I hate divorce," says the Lord God Almighty. Too often we perceive those words spoken in condemning judgment. But look closely at the context in which they were written. We find that Judah had "desecrated the sanctuary the Lord loves, by marrying the daughter of a foreign God" (2:11). God's *bride* had given herself to someone else. Judah had tossed aside the glorious future of a relationship with her faithful God for another lover. Judah replied to God's loving acts and caring with the words, "We're getting a divorce."

God's guts were ripped out. Couldn't they see?! Didn't they know?! What more could they want than the perfect love of God the Father? How could they reject His perfect gift for such a cheap imitation? God was in great pain. And God knows that pain today. He feels it every time His people reject His love, when we go our own way, when we "marry the daughter of a foreign God." God hates divorce because it hurts. It hurts Him. It hurts His children.

Bible Text

He gives strength to the weary and increases the power of the weak. Even youths grow tired and weary, and young men stumble and fall; but those who hope in the Lord will renew their strength. They will soar on wings like eagles; they will run and not grow weary, they will walk and not be faint

(Isaiah 40:29–31).

From the beginning, God has joined Himself to us through a promise (Gen. 17:7–8). From the beginning God created marriage to join a man and a woman. The relationship between husband and wife is intended as an inviolable covenant. It is an earthly reflection of God's covenant with His people. (See Matt. 19:4–6.)

Divorce not only destroys family relationships but also shatters our understanding of the permanency of the covenant. The covenant between husband and wife is the strongest commitment we can make. It is our pledge, "in sickness and in health, for richer and for poorer, for better and for worse … till death do us part." God compares His covenant with us to this marriage commitment (Hosea 2:19–20).

> Divorce shatters our understanding of the permanency of the covenant.

It is no wonder that when the marriage pledge is broken between husband and wife, they are hit with a flood of emotions. Guilt, shame, pain, anger, humiliation, and a host of other feelings replace the love, peace, and security that the covenant was designed to bring. In divorce we feel the sting of sin, of brokenness in our relationship with God, as well as with a spouse.

Yet God, who cries out, "I hate divorce," is the same God who compassionately promises, "I have loved you with an everlasting love; I have drawn you with loving-kindness. I will build you up again and you will be rebuilt, O Virgin Israel" (Jer. 31:3–4). What a powerful passage of healing love! Regardless of the cause of the divorce, our Father promises to rebuild and restore His people, seeing them again as "Virgin Israel."

God reminds us that His faithfulness is not dependent on ours (2 Tim. 2:13). God has made a vow to us based solely on His goodness and His love. In Jesus Christ He extended that love to us through the sacrifice of His only Son. The cross is the symbol of God's faithful love toward us. "He Himself bore our sins in His body on the tree, so that we might die to sins and live for righteousness; by His wounds you have been healed" (1 Peter 2:24).

Our God is a God who hates divorce but loves His people with an everlasting love. In Jesus Christ we see the depth of His love—a love that calls us to be faithful in marriage as He is faithful, and a love that removes sin from our lives and replaces it with His compassion and healing.

Prayer

Spend time thinking about God's powerful, unconditional everlasting love. Ask God to help you understand and live in the confidence of that love. Lift up anyone you know who is affected by divorce so that they too will come to know and experience God's everlasting love.

For Further Study

Divorce is a sensitive issue. On the one hand, God declares His opposition to divorce; on the other, He holds out healing and reconciliation to those affected by it. As members of His body, we also are called to share the Gospel with those affected by divorce. The following verses help guide a response for those affected by divorce.

Rom. 8:38–39—There is no depth where God's love doesn't reach.

Rom. 5:8—God demonstrates His love toward sinners.

Heb. 10:23—God is faithful.

Ps. 103—God offers forgiveness and healing.

Matt. 11:28—Jesus is rest for the weary.

For Reflection

1. Consider the number and variety of feelings people must experience when going through a divorce. What emotions do you think children involved in divorce feel?

2. How is your relationship with God strengthened by the realization that He loves you with an everlasting love?

3. How can you help those affected by divorce, especially the young people you teach or know, experience God's acceptance, forgiveness, and love?

See Power Plays, Book 1, Study 9—"What Now, God?"

What Does God Want from Me?

When it comes right down to it, many of life's questions can be boiled down to one: "What does God want?" Youth and adults alike struggle to discover God's purpose for them. It is a question that God's children have asked since the beginning of time!

Paul prays for the Colossians to "live a life worthy of the Lord" and to "please Him in every way." People often ask how this is possible since we are all sinners. Paul would not have prayed such a prayer unless he believed it was possible. In fact, he goes on to list four specific ways that his readers, then and now, could live such a "worthy" life.

First, believers bear fruit in every good work. The Bible is filled with this imagery—Jesus spoke of reward in heaven for good deeds on earth (Matt. 16:27). The "fruit of the Spirit" (Gal. 5:22) is a basic memory text for Christians. Even the prophet Isaiah used the word picture of a fruitful vineyard to describe God's faithful people (Is. 27:2–6). This fruit is not the result of striving on the part of the branch, but a natural result of the branch's connection to the life-giving tree (John 15:4–5).

Second, believers grow in the knowledge of God. Students of all ages learn well the tasks of studying, taking tests, listening to lectures, performing experiments, and practicing repeatedly to grow in knowledge. Likewise, Christians are familiar with studying the Word, testing their knowledge in life situations, listening to preaching, serving others, and worshipping repeatedly.

Third, believers are marked by a great endurance and patience in the face of suffering. My father entered his eternal

Bible Text

And we pray this in order that you may live a life worthy of the Lord and may please Him in every way: bearing fruit in every good work, growing in the knowledge of God, being strengthened with all power according to His glorious might so that you may have great endurance and patience, and joyfully giving thanks to the Father, who has qualified you to share in the inheritance of the saints in the kingdom of light **(Colossians 1:10–12).**

> Believers bear fruit in every good work.

glory after suffering for almost nine years with cancer. Most of that time, especially toward the end of his earthly life, Dad endured physical and emotional pain as the disease spread and he faced his death. His doctors and nurses often questioned his faith, wondering why "his God" would allow such suffering. What affected them profoundly was Dad's constant hope, serenity, and cheer throughout his illness and as he died. I praise God for Dad's powerful witness to the Lord's love and care.

Finally, believers acknowledge with joy and thankfulness what God has done for them. In Corrie Ten Boom's book, *The Hiding Place*, she relates how, amid the squalor of a Nazi concentration camp, her sister questioned God's command to give thanks in all circumstances. The sisters' thanks became genuine when they realized that the biting fleas and the putrid smell kept the guards from searching their barracks and finding their Bible, allowing them freedom to study, worship, and witness with less fear.

Despite all of this overwhelming evidence that God is pleased when His people live a worthy life, we still struggle with the concept of *worthiness*, since we know that our good works cannot earn God's favor or merit salvation. We must therefore look back to the *source* of power in all these examples. To bear fruit, one must be connected to the Vine, Jesus. To grow in knowledge of God, the Spirit must first impart it (1 Cor. 12:3). To endure with patience, one must be strengthened with the power of God. To joyfully give thanks to the Father, one must first experience His grace. Paul ends this passage by reminding us that our worthiness lies in being qualified by God to share the saint's inheritance. It is simply our reaction to *God's* action.

God's purpose, then, is for you and me to bear the fruit of good works, grow in knowledge of Him, patiently endure trials, and witness to our joy and thanks for all He has done for us, *all through faith in Jesus Christ*. Looking back, we might even rephrase the question, "What does God want *for* me?" He stands ready to give us more than we could imagine or request.

> Lord, thanks for all You have given me. Help me be ready to give it all back to You.

Prayer

Lord, thanks for all You have given me. Help me be ready to give it all back to You. Forgive the feebleness of my efforts and sinful motives. Strengthen me for Your service and give me opportunities to serve. Amen.

For Further Study

Profitable material to further explore this issue is the book of Job. Scan chapters 1–3, browse Job's dialog with his friends (or read it thoroughly, if you wish), and check out the final chapters. Job's final acceptance that God's plans are best is recorded in Job 42:1–6.

God's plans for us may include times of testing and trial as well as times of joy.

For Reflection

1. Recall one or two examples of good works that you have done recently. What was good about them?

2. Think of a time when you experienced suffering of any kind, small or great. Did you endure it patiently, protest it vehemently, or react somewhere in between?

3. Look at your answers to the previous two questions. Do they remind you of selfish motives and sinful ways? Take a moment now to confess and repent of them. Do they celebrate God's power and grace in your life? Take time to praise God for His goodness.

Simple People with an Awesome Message

> **See Power Plays, Book 1, Study 10—**
> "Good News for Your Friends"

God could have done it Himself. He could have skipped all the hassles, failures, and disappointments. Why God chose people to spread His Word and build His kingdom is puzzling. That the all-perfect, holy God should put His all-perfect, holy message into the care of sinful, defiant, rebellious, stiff-necked people is a mystery.

It certainly puzzled Moses. You probably know the story from Exodus 4. Moses, heir-apparent to the Egyptian throne, now hides out in the desert. One day he gets a flaming fax from God: "I am sending you to Pharaoh to bring My people the Israelites out of Egypt" (Ex. 3:10). What happens next shows us what was really inside of Moses. What we see is not exactly the stuff of heroes. Time and again Moses tries to worm his way out of God's call and each time God insists.

Yet, if we jump to the final chapter of the book of Deuteronomy, we read, "Since then, no prophet has risen in Israel like Moses, whom the LORD knew face to face. ... For no one has ever shown the mighty power or performed the awesome deeds that Moses did in the sight of all Israel" (Deut. 34:10–12).

A couple of questions pop up: "Why didn't God just speak directly to the people instead of using Moses?" "What happened that turned Moses from a man of doubt to a performer of awesome deeds?"

The first is one of those questions the Scriptures do not directly address. As we look through Israel's history, we see human failure, stubbornness, and outright rebellion. As we look at the history of the New Testament and the church through the past two thousand years, we find much the same result. We see God's Word misused, abused, and cited as rational for any number of ungodly atrocities. Relying on humans seems like a bad idea.

Bible Text

The LORD said to him, "Who gave man his mouth? Who makes him deaf or dumb? Who gives him sight or makes him blind? Is it not I, the Lord? Now go; I will help you speak and teach you what to say" **(Exodus 4:11–12).**

26

We get an insight into why God chooses to work through sinful people in 2 Cor. 4:7 where Paul declares, "We have this treasure in jars of clay to show that this all-surpassing power is from God and not from us." Maybe the best hope for a lowly jar of clay is another jar of clay. Maybe the best one to reach a bunch of doubting, resistant people is a doubting, resistant shepherd.

The analogy is fitting for you and me today. Maybe the best way God can reach lost sheep is through sometimes doubting, sometimes rebellious, sometimes stiff-necked sheep who know a saving Shepherd. For whatever reason, God has seen it best to include you and me in spreading the Good News, in working with Him to seek and save the lost—an awesome task for ill-equipped people.

As for question 2, "What happened to Moses to turn him into such a fireball?" The key is in our text. God assured Moses, "I will help you speak and will teach you what to say." God Himself was the power behind Moses' words. The effectiveness of Moses' witness was not in his finely-prepared speech, well-rehearsed testimony, or gregarious personality. Moses spoke and people listened because the Spirit of God worked through him.

Well, that's great for Moses, but what about you and me? When it comes to "witnessing," what will keep us from offending people, from turning them off, or sounding like a fanatic? What happens if they won't listen and won't believe? The answer is the same that God gave to Moses: "That's not your concern. I will be the power behind your words." Paul affirms this in Rom. 1:16, "I am not ashamed of the gospel, because it is the power of God for the salvation of everyone who believes." The power to change doubting and rebellious hearts is in the Gospel. God's Word brings life as it is shared through the words and lives of His sheep. The power behind our testimony is not how well we live, in how persuasively we speak, or in the great spiritual things we might do. The real power is in God's Word.

Moses was a clay jar. Yet he is remembered as the greatest prophet of God. Among his last recorded words are these which point to source of his focus, "Blessed are you, O Israel! Who is like you, a people saved by the Lord? He is your shield and helper and your glorious sword" (Deut. 38:29). Moses realized he was a simple man with an awesome God who had some words for him to share.

We too realize we are simple people. And we, like Moses, need to focus on our awesome God and the powerful words He has given us to share—the Gospel of Jesus Christ.

Prayer

Consider some of the things that intimidate you about sharing your faith. Ask God to strengthen your trust in the power of His Word. Then ask God to bring to your mind fitting ways to share your faith.

For Further Study

God calls us, ready or not, as His disciples to be involved in His work of seeking and saving the lost. For many, that thought brings perspiration and panic. Putting our focus on God and the power of the Gospel can overcome fear and self-doubts.

The following verses will sharpen your focus:

Heb. 4:12—We have the power of the living and active Word.

2 Tim. 3:16—We have the assurance of God's inspired Word.

Rom. 10:17—Faith comes through the Word.

Philemon 6—Talking about our faith results in many blessings.

Ps. 19:7-11—God's Word has power.

1 Peter 2:9—We are called by God to declare His praise to others.

For Reflection

1. When you think of "witnessing," what images come to mind?

2. What are some things that are intimidating about sharing the Gospel?

3. God was pretty creative in the ways He got His message across in the Old Testament. What are creative ways you might share your faith with those around you?

See Power Plays, Book 1, Study 11—

"What Comes First?"

The King and I

Have you ever played "King of the Mountain"? One person establishes himself at the top of a mound of dirt and declares himself "king." Then all the other players storm up the hill attempting to knock the "king" over and take his place. Usually no one gets to be "king" very long. The position is always challenged and the defender inevitably falls.

Becoming king sounds like a great idea. Kings have power, prestige, and unlimited resources. Kings can do whatever they want. A king is number 1—the greatest—the top of the heap. But most kings have a limited reign. Kings look over their shoulders a lot because somebody else (usually number 2) wants to be number 1.

Kings also have a lot of responsibility. When anything goes wrong in the kingdom, the king gets blamed. It is, obviously, his fault. Whenever a king's subject needs help, he petitions the king. The king is responsible for the care of his people. When the enemy rides up over the ridge, the king gets summoned. It's his job to protect his kingdom. When a king is given gifts or shown affection, he never knows if the gestures are sincere or if they are merely attempts to gain his favor. Who would want to be king, anyway?

Being God is even worse. Oh, it sounds good—all-powerful, all-knowing, recipient of praise and offerings, the Greatest—the Ultimate Number One—the King of kings. But being God can be a real pain.

> God gives His children good and perfect gifts, about which they complain or waste.
>
> He answers every petition according to His ultimate wisdom, but is second-guessed and angrily told how He could have done it better.
>
> He protects His subjects from great calamities, and then gets grumbled at because of minor discomforts.
>
> For the good of all, He establishes rules that are then ignored or distorted, jeopardizing the very people He wants to protect.

Bible Text

"This is the covenant I will make with the house of Israel after that time," declares the LORD. "I will put My law in their minds and write it on their hearts. I will be their God, and they will be My people. No longer will a man teach his neighbor, or a man his brother, saying, 'Know the Lord,' because they will all know Me, from the least of them to the greatest," declares the LORD. "For I will forgive their wickedness and will remember their sins no more" **(Jeremiah 31:33–34).**

He asks only loyalty and love, but receives half-hearted acknowledgement that He even exists.

Then there are the challengers—those who think they would rather be God, those who think they could do a better job than the One who created them in the first place.

Striving to be "King of the Mountain" is a challenge. But real life is no game. God who sits in the heavens with earth as His footstool will not be usurped.

God took the responsibility as our loving Father-Creator to care for His people. He sees us scrambling up our man-made hills shouting in His face. When we rebel against Him, breaking the relationship He had instituted, He reaches out to restore us.

Jer. 31:34–35 describes what happens when God's people do acknowledge His Kingship and live in their place in His Kingdom. God forgives His people, and remembers their sins no more. He institutes a very unique kingdom based not on nationality or edict, but on a covenant—His unbreakable promise.

The old kingdom was based on a set of rules—the Law, the Commandments. But the very first of the laws, the basis of all the rest, was seemingly impossible to obey. "You shall have no other gods before Me!"

The new kingdom described in Jer. 31:34–35 is based on an act of God. "You win!" He declares. "I am your God because I have decided it. I have won you in battle, and it is finished. You are Mine! I *am* first in your heart. I put Myself there when you were baptized, when you became My own."

Little children sometimes pout when they are upset, "I won't be your child (friend) any more." But wise parents know that a few angry words do not change the relationship that exists. So too our empty challenges of God's authority over our lives may cause us some discomfort and may grieve the heart of our King. But His covenant is in place. It will not be broken.

Protected by that wonderful covenant, we respond to our great and almighty God. He motivates and empowers us to live in His Kingdom as His loyal subjects, demonstrating our faithfulness to Him each day.

Because of Jesus, the King of Calvary's Mountain, we have our place within this great covenant, and worship our one, true God with all our hearts, all our souls, and all our lives.

Prayer

Pray for the leaders in our nation and world. Ask God to give them wisdom and a desire to know and do His will.

Pray for people who live in countries without human rights or godly leaders.

Thank God for being who He is and for the certainty that He will honor His covenant of love and forgiveness with you.

For Further Study

These passages may expand your understanding of idolatry:

Ex. 20:3–17—Transgressing each commandment involves breaking also the first.

Is. 48:11—God will not share His glory.

Matt. 22:34–40—Jesus' summary of God's Word begins with loving God wholeheartedly.

For Reflection

1. Draw a picture of God to reflect His attributes. For example, you might draw several large arms to symbolize His strength. How would you illustrate His feelings toward people?

2. God made people in His image. In what way(s) are you like God?

3. Make a time line of your life, starting with your birth, on which you graph your faith life. On what occasions did your faith increase? When did it seem weak? In another color superimpose the reality of God's care for you during those years. How do you know His care was constant?

4. Would you like to be a king? What would you do if you were in charge of this world? What problems would you expect to encounter? If you couldn't assume that role, who would you want to be in that position?

See Power Plays, Book 1, Study 12—

"The Dark Side"

Satan, Lord of Darkness

We live in a world of growing darkness. Many in our society no longer view things as either right or wrong. We are caught up in an era that says that there are no absolutes, only generalities. No black or white, only gray. No right or wrong, only expedience and experience. As one student remarked, "Cheating is okay. It doesn't really hurt anyone, and with my schedule, I don't really have all that much time for studying. It's not like I'm going out and killing anybody." We build schedules for ourselves that overfill our time and add more stress than joy. We are tempted to entertain ourselves with movies, music, and video simulations that promote violence, unbridled sexuality, and abuse. Subjects and views that were once only whispered between adults are broadcast on prime-time TV. We see people—adults, teenagers, and even children—express anger and attempt to resolve arguments with guns.

Paul's "god of this age," the prince of darkness, is, indeed, alive and well on planet Earth and is gaining subtle control of many of the things that are a part of a everyday life. Satan must laugh as we fall once again for the old tricks and temptations that have tripped up God's people from the beginning.

Even curriculums within our schools are not immune to the subtleties of Satan. In 1993, a curriculum was introduced on a trial basis to a school in Southern California that encouraged youth to meditate, in a classroom atmosphere, and open their minds to a "spirit friend." New Age concepts of this kind are becoming more and more accepted within the framework of our young peoples' education.

Bible Text

The god of this age [Satan] has blinded the minds of unbelievers, so that they cannot see the light of the gospel of the glory of Christ, who is the image of God. For we do not preach ourselves, but Jesus Christ as Lord, and ourselves as your servants for Jesus' sake. For God, who said, "Let light shine out of darkness," made His light shine in our hearts to give us the light of the knowledge of the glory of God in the face of Christ **(2 Corinthians 4:4–6).**

> Satan must laugh as we fall once again for the old tricks and temptations that have tripped up God's people from the beginning.

We may at times be lulled into a sense of security, failing to see Satan at work around us and in us. Or we may be acutely aware of the devil's work and power and be led to despair. In a world that becomes more and more frightening and in which the devil seems to become more and more prominent, the good news is that we have a changeless Christ in our ever-changing world. God does not mince words when He warns us of the power of Satan. We are warned in 1 Peter 5:8, "Be self-controlled and alert. Your enemy the devil prowls around like a roaring lion looking for someone to devour." But God also has provided a certain means of protection for us. "For God, who said, 'Let light shine out of darkness,' made His light shine in our hearts to give us the light of the knowledge of the glory of God in the face of Christ" (2 Cor. 4:6).

God has sent His Son, Jesus Christ, to be a light for our world. We are not immune to Satan's temptations. We do not leave or ignore the darkness of the world around us. But those who share faith in Christ see and are His light in the world. We are armed to oppose Satan with the gifts God gives in His grace (Eph. 6:10ff). As we share in Christ's suffering and death through our Baptism, we have His light in our hearts, reminding us of the forgiveness of our sins and the power we have for new life. Even when we fall into the devil's tempting snares, or stumble into the darkness of his world, we are secure. Satan's power is not a match for God's unconditional love.

> God does not mince words when He warns us of the power of Satan.

Prayer

Spend time in prayer guided by the following suggestions:

Pray to be sensitive to the darkness that impacts us on a daily basis.
Pray for strength to make sound decisions and to guide others to make good choices.
Thank God for His love that empowers and protects you.
Pray that you may be a Christlike example, a light, to those you serve.

For Further Study

For a deeper look at Scripture's teaching about Satan and Christ's power over him, consider these passages.

Matt. 24:24; Mark 13:5; Col. 2:8—Jesus speaks of false prophets/deceivers.

Mark 4:15—Satan is a thief of souls.

2 Cor. 11:14–15; Matt. 7:15—Satan is the deceiver.

Is. 9:2; John 1:1–5; 3:17–21; 8:12—Jesus came to dispel the darkness.

Matt. 11:28–30—Jesus will carry our burdens.

Rom. 13:12; Acts 26:17–18 [God speaks to Paul]; Is. 58:9–11—As children of the light, we can be people of action.

For Reflection

1. Think back over the last week and the TV shows you viewed. How many Christian values can you list that were portrayed?

2. What computer and video games are currently popular? What are their themes? What is their appeal?

3. What might you say to someone—youth or adult—who expresses doubt about the existence or power of Satan?

4. What are the best sources in your life for **light** from God? How could you share more **light** with those you meet, teach, or live with?

UNIT 2

See Power Plays, Book 2, Study 1—
"I Can Help!"

Love Me, Love My Problems?

We've all been there before—you're on your way out the door, or up to your graying hair in an important project, and a friend interrupts with a hopeful, "Can we talk?" Something in your friend's tone immediately lets you know that this will take time—time you don't have. Or maybe you *do* have time—time to yourself, the first day in weeks to spend relaxing alone or with your family, and someone encroaches on that precious time to discuss at length a problem he or she is experiencing. You are torn between a willingness to help and the desire to hide.

These scenarios are common. Adults and youth alike face them, sometimes routinely. How can we be empowered to respond as Christians to these demands? John points to the answer in 1 John 3:16–18.

Verse 16 immediately defines the issue for us—*love* is the ultimate goal. We know what that entails through the example of Jesus, the Good Shepherd who lays down His life for the sheep (John 10:11). The shepherd's primary concern was his flock. All others were of secondary importance. We learn from Jesus that another person's need should be a top priority for us if we are to communicate God's love.

A local Christian radio station reported a little boy who was asked if he would donate blood for his older sister, who needed his rare type for life-saving surgery. The little boy trembled at the thought, but after thinking about his sister, he consented. His mother held his hand during the procedure, as the boy's terror was obvious. Final-

> **Bible Text**
> This is how we know what love is: Jesus Christ laid down His life for us. And we ought to lay down our lives for our brothers. If anyone has material possessions and sees his brother in need but has no pity on him, how can the love of God be in him? Dear children, let us not love with words or tongue but with actions and in truth **(1 John 3:16–18).**

> We learn from Jesus that another person's need should be a top priority for us if we are to communicate God's love.

ly, the nurse leaned over and said, "We are all done; thank you for giving your blood for your sister." The boy looked at his mother with tears in his eyes and asked, "Mommy, when do I die?"

God's love is that kind of sacrificial love. His Son suffered and died on our behalf. As Christ lives in us, we too can display that sacrificial love. That kind of love prompts us to give our friend's problem 100% of our attention and empathy.

Verse 17 reveals the source of this love, as well as the evidence of its presence. It is the love of God, that lives in the heart of the believer by the power of the Holy Spirit (Romans 5:5). Without it we cannot respond to our friend's need, no matter how hard we try. With it we can generously give ourselves away to our friends, without resentment at feeling imposed upon or expecting anything in return. Here John refers specifically to material needs and sharing, but the principle also applies to other responses to another's need—such as lending a listening ear or taking time out of the day in order to help our friends.

In a world still plagued by sin, our ability to consistently reflect God's love will be imperfect. When we fail to respond to a friend's need with love, we may be tempted to believe that God really doesn't live in us. But John is quick to remind us earlier in chapter 2, verse 1, that "we have one who speaks to the Father in our defense—Jesus Christ, the Righteous One." We can go to Him in repentance and faith to receive full forgiveness, as well as the power to put our love into action next time.

Verse 18 is a wonderful exhortation to "put our money where our mouths are" when it comes to loving others. Does this mean that we should always be able to drop everything and respond immediately when a friend has a need? Probably not—we can quickly become a doormat instead of a servant, and love will become very scarce in our lives. A friend will sense when our attempt at loving help is not genuine. Sometimes, a response such as, "I'm afraid that I cannot give you the attention you deserve right now; can we talk after lunch instead?" may be the most honest, loving answer we can give.

When we are called upon to help someone or asked for our advice, there can also be tremendous pressure to "fix" everything

For Further Study

Job 2:11 ff; Job 32:3 ff—The book of Job describes the efforts (mostly unhelpful) of Job's friends to assist him in a time of trial.

Prov. 18:24 and Prov. 27:6—Solomon gives this pair of proverbs on friendship.

John 15:13–14—Jesus describes His friendship with us and shows the length to which a friend will go for someone, as Christ Himself did, even giving His life for us. While our sinful human nature keeps us from following Christ's example perfectly, it is both an example and source of power for us in our friendships with others.

> With God's strength, we can witness to His love in us, by choosing appropriate times, words, and actions in responses to the immediate problems or needs of our friends.

For Reflection

1. What competes for our attention toward a friend in need? Are there other issues equally important?

2. Think about two or three blessings you have that can help respond to a friend in need. They might be material things, spiritual gifts, or other special abilities God has given you. (For example, David played his harp to comfort King Saul; Nathan confronted David with his sin, and David was led to repent, etc.)

3. What can you do when a friend's problem is too big to handle? List three responses that will communicate love.

or solve the problem at hand. If we *can* help, then praise the Lord! More often, however, we feel helpless or inadequate, especially in the face of seemingly insurmountable trials, such as divorce, psychological or physical illness, or death. A young person for instance, might experience depression, drug abuse, a broken home, and repeated appearances in juvenile court. We cannot necessarily fix everything, but we can listen, make counseling referrals, visit detention centers, keep in touch with probation officers and caseworkers by phone to pledge support, and above all, *pray* for the youth's family.

With God's strength, we can witness to His love in us, by choosing appropriate times, words, and actions in responses to the immediate problems or needs of our friends. Then we can love, not just "with words or tongue, but with actions and in truth."

Prayer

Dear Lord, I love because You first loved me. When friends need me, let me be there for them, as I would respond to You. Amen.

See Power Plays, Book 2, Study 2—

"The Price of Popularity"

Popularity

At the end of each year *People* magazine features the most popular people for that particular year. The list consists of superstars, people in high positions, athletes, achievers, stars, and starlets. They are people who have usually excelled in ability, intelligence, achievement, or beauty. The world has usually heard or seen these people throughout the year on television or radio. But each year most of these "popular" people are replaced by others. Popularity is at best fickle! "Here today, gone tomorrow!" is a slogan that can certainly apply to stardom.

Though popularity is changeable, it remains a driving force for many people, especially young people. People want to be accepted. They want approval. They want to be included. They want to be invited. They want to be wanted.

There's certainly nothing wrong with desiring to be wanted and included—to be popular. There *is* something wrong, though, when popularity requires compromising or reducing one's values. Popularity can be very expensive. Good people will even do bad things to be popular. St. Paul struggled over the same thing as he asked, "Am I now trying to win the approval of men, or of God? Or am I trying to please men?" (Gal. 1:10).

Jesus was popular—at times. Repeatedly, people pressed Him for healing. They sought Him out (John 6:24). They cried out for His attention. In many respects, He was extremely popular. Had there been a *Time* magazine during Jesus' time, Jesus might have been "Man of the Year." After feeding the 5000, the people wanted to force Him to be their king, but He refused (John 6:14–15). However, that was not the kind of popularity He wanted.

Bible Text

But you are a chosen people, a royal priesthood, a holy nation, a people belonging to God, that you may declare the praises of Him who called you out of darkness into His wonderful light. Once you were not a people, but now you are the people of God; once you had not received mercy, but now you have received mercy (1 Peter 2:9–10).

> In His unpopularity—"Crucify Him, Crucify Him"—we became popular with God.

For Further Study

1. Study other passages that make us aware of how valuable we are in God's eyes. These include Rom. 8:33–34; Eph. 1:3–4; 4:21–24; 5:25 –27; Col. 1:22; 1 Peter 1:15–19.

2. Review your high school yearbook. Who was most popular? Who was elected queen? Who were the jocks? Are they still "popular"? Are they successful? As you reflect, pray for those you think about.
3. Read **Christ Esteem: Where the Search for Self-Esteem Ends** (© 1990 Harvest House Publishers) by Dr. Don Matzat. It suggests that personal fulfillment is never found in ourselves but only in Jesus Christ.

For Reflection

1. Why would it be difficult for the readers of Peter's epistle to see themselves as "... royal ... holy ... a people belonging to God"? Why is it difficult for us to see ourselves as described in 1 Peter 2:9–10?
2. Look up the definition of popularity in the dictionary. In what ways does or does not 1 Peter 2:9–10 match up to the definition given in the dictionary?
3. What privileges and responsibilities come along with the honors God has bestowed upon us according to 1 Peter 2:11–12?
4. How can we meet the popularity needs of young people or adults whom we serve?

For Jesus it was most important to be obedient to His Father's will—to redeem humanity from sin, death, and the power of the devil. Jesus could do this only by fulfilling the Law perfectly for us and paying the price we deserve for our sin—death. On the Mount of Olives He prayed in great agony, "… not My will, but Yours be done" (Luke 22:42). He, a perfect Son, became unpopular, forsaken even by God, in order to rescue us. In His unpopularity—"Crucify Him, Crucify Him"—we became popular with God. Our sins no longer separate us from Him. Eternal life was given back to us.

> As people of God, the honor of eternity is ours.

Our popularity is accentuated in 1 Peter 2:9–10. In verse 9, St. Peter speaks words similar to those Moses spoke to the Israelites in Ex. 19:5–6. Both Peter and Moses remind the people that they are God's special people—children of God's grace. Through Jesus Christ we, New Testament people, are God's "chosen people" just as the Israelites were God's chosen people in the Old Testament. We are a "royal priesthood, a holy nation, a people belonging to God, that [we] may declare the praises of Him who called [us] out of darkness and into His wonderful light" (1 Peter 2:9). Talk about being popular. Special. We are "holy," separated out to reflect the very character of God. How could anyone be more important? We were "once … not a people," meaning we were of Gentile ancestry, but now we are the very "people of God" (1 Peter 2:10). As people of God, the honor of eternity is ours. Someday, before all of creation we will be acknowledged as God's dear children: "Come, you who are blessed by My Father; take your inheritance, the kingdom prepared for you since the creation of the world" (Matt. 25:34). Could there be any greater honor?

Prayer

Spend a few minutes in prayer using the acronym ACTS as a guide.

Adoration. Give adoration to God for having chosen you, making you a "royal priesthood, a holy nation, people belonging to God."

Confession. Confess your sin of sometimes compromising or forgetting values in order to be popular.

Thanksgiving. Give thanks to God for the gift of His Son, Jesus Christ, who became unpopular so you might become popular with God.

Supplication. Pray for those with whom you come into contact that you might help them see their value because of the sacrificial life, death, and resurrection of Jesus Christ.

See Power Plays, Book 2, Study 3—"When Friends Make Me Choose"

Divided Loyalties between Friends

Friends—we all search for them, adults and teens alike. We all long to have friends and be friends to others. As human beings we long for a kinship with others of our kind. In these relationships, we strive to be the best friend we can be and we put a great deal of trust into those people we label as our "best friends." When we feel that one of our friends has betrayed us, the results can be devastating and at the very least, incredibly painful. We rely on our friends to be confidants, advisors, and companions. Especially for teens, loyalty to friends is one of the strongest forces in their lives.

Some friendships can have a negative influence upon the lives of teens. Some inflict permanent harm. An example of such a case is Julie. Julie was not popular at school. She was painfully shy, didn't have much money, and her clothes were not the current fashion. She usually sat by herself during the school lunch period. She didn't participate in any school activities. Jane, on the other hand, was extremely popular and always out for a lark. On a dare, she befriended Julie and began to spend time with her. Julie was ecstatic. At last she had found someone important who cared about her. She followed Jane around like a puppy.

After a few weeks, Jane's circle of friends became bored with what they had termed "the Julie game." They decided to take their game one step further. It would be fun to see what would happen if they got Julie drunk. Jane invited Julie to one of the parties that she often attended—no parental supervision and lots of alcohol. Julie didn't even hesitate. In her mind, an invitation meant that she was finally completely accepted by Jane's crowd. At the party,

Bible Text

If we live, we live to the Lord; if we die, we die to the Lord. So, whether we live or we die, we belong to the Lord. For this very reason, Christ died and returned to life so that He might be the Lord of both the dead and the living. You, then, why do you judge your brother? Or why do you look down on your brother? For we will all stand before God's judgment seat **(Romans 14:8–10).**

> ... [young people] will have a much better chance of surviving events that seem life-shattering to them if they have Christ at the helm of their lives.

For Further Study

1. There are over 150 references to friends/friendship in God's Word. The following Bible verses offer a variety of incidences of both good and bad relationships:

   1 Sam. 18:1–4; 20:42; 2 Sam. 1—We see God's gift of loyal friendship between Jonathan and David.

   Ex. 33:11; 2 Chron. 20:7; Is. 41:8; James 2:23—God demonstrates friendship with Abraham.

   Job 16:20–21—Job talks about the loyalty of friends.

   Prov. 19:4, 6; 2 Kings 10:11; Ps. 109:4–5—Beware of false friendships.

   Prov. 17:17—The love of a friend is described.

   Matt. 26:50; John 11:11—Jesus is a friend.

Jane led Julie to experiment with alcohol. Julie was hesitant at first but, with a little encouragement, joined in with growing enthusiasm. She found that the alcohol made her feel warm, comfortable, and accepted.

The day after the party, Jane seemed to totally lose interest in Julie. Jane didn't want to be a friend any longer. Julie was devastated. She retreated into a world of loneliness and fear. In her depression, she remembered how good the alcohol had made her feel at the party. Julie began to drink, and alcohol soon became her closest friend. She became entangled in a downward spiral of drinking and despair.

Julie is not the only victim in this story. Jane too is a victim. Popularity and peer pressure were important things in her life. Her need to be popular with and attractive to others stemmed from fear of rejection and masked emotional distress.

Our young people's lives are fractured by sin. The choices that they make in their friendships can last a lifetime or destroy their lives. Teenagers find it so hard to like and accept themselves. They rely heavily on others to tell them how good they are or how bad they are. Because of sin, their values can become distorted. Their relationships are sometimes based on the wrong set of parameters.

Unfortunately, neither of the girls in the above scenario knew a Savior who could help them through this time. This is not to say that all teenagers who are grounded in Christ will not have problems of this type. But they will have a much better chance of surviving events that seem life-shattering to them if they have Christ at the helm of their lives. Christ invites us in Matt. 11:28 to "Come to me, all you who are weary and burdened, and I will give you rest."

> By God's grace we can help others recognize their uniqueness and become more aware of a Savior who is real and active in their lives.

By God's grace we can help others recognize their uniqueness and become more aware of a Savior who is real and active in their lives. These things happen as we share God's grace with them. We want to help them discover the life-long friendship that Jesus Christ has to offer, and we want them to like and believe in themselves. Then they will be better prepared to make correct choices in all areas of their lives.

In John 15:14 Jesus calls us friends. Just prior to this statement He says, "Greater love has no one than this, that he lay down his life for his friends." Jesus called us His friends and then died on a cross to set us free. As leaders and teachers of youth, it is imperative that we make sure that teens know of the wonderful grace of our Lord and His free gift of redemption.

Sadly, even adults have a difficult time relating to the unbounded love of our God. 67% of those who were asked how to get to heaven responded by affirming the statement, "I believe I must obey God's rules and commandments in order to be saved" (*Effective Christian Education: Summary Report,* Minneapolis: Search Institute, 1990, p. 69). How can we teach something that we have a hard time accepting ourselves? Psalm 139 tells about our intimate relationship with God. "For You created my inmost being; you knit me together in my mother's womb" (v. 13). Our God loves us beyond all reason.

We hear much today about the gangs that are running rampant within our cities. The core of gang mentality is the need to belong, to be accepted. In a world of confusion and bitterness, we all need to know that we have a friend who truly understands. We are important and special in God's eyes. In Matt. 26:50, Jesus calls Judas His friend, even as Judas betrays Him. He is our friend, today, tomorrow, and always—never changing, ever faithful, loving in all circumstances, and offering eternal life through His resurrection.

Prayer

Lord, help me to be a friend to those I serve. Help me provide guidance and comfort to each of those whose lives I touch, so that they may stand in love and in courage surrounded by the strength that only You can provide. Help me to share my vulnerability with them, that they may understand that we are not so very far apart. Most of all, help me to show to them a friendship that will last for all time—a friendship with You. Amen.

For Reflection

1. Think of someone who has been a good friend. What are the qualities in that friend that you most admire? Why did you seek his/her friendship?

2. Think of a time when a friend was disloyal. Reflect on your feelings at that time.

3. Read Ps. 100 and consider the friendship that we have with our God. Spend time mentally listing the qualities of this type of friendship.

4. How might you counsel a teenager who seems caught up in friendships that could harm his or her faith or compromise his or her values?

See Power Plays, Book 2, Study 4—

"What Will I Do with My Life?"

Career Decisions

Children and young people are often asked, "What do you want to be when you grow up?" That question has undoubtedly been asked thousands of times during this century alone. It may appear innocent, harmless, and even intriguing, but it can be a confusing question in our current complex society.

The common answers to this question center on the future profession or job that an individual might desire—firefighter, teacher, lawyer, ball player, pastor, etc. Those answers subtly shift from the original question that was not "What do you want to *be* when you grow up?" but "What do you want to *do*?" There is a distinct difference between *being* and *doing*. It is an important difference to note, especially as we attempt to help young people clarify their future careers and adult life responsibilities.

So much of life today centers around *doing*. The focus on doing is a natural one for us to have. We wake each morning with an agenda of what we must do to make it through the day. Children, even at an early age, are given tasks to complete. Throughout life we gain satisfaction accomplishing our tasks. What we do can earn us money, allow us to acquire possessions, and establish a lifestyle that makes us comfortable. Doing has its place, but if overdone, it can be harmful, both physically and spiritually.

We need to balance knowing who we are (being) and what we are about (doing). Who we are is a more elusive concept than *what we do*. We do not discover who we are by completing long "to do" lists. In fact, people who have spent a great deal of time *doing*

> **We need to balance knowing who we are (being) and what we are about (doing).**

Bible Text

No one will be able to stand up against you all the days of your life. As I was with Moses, so I will be with you; I will never leave you or forsake you. Be strong and courageous, because you will lead these people to inherit the land I swore to their forefathers to give them. Be strong and very courageous. Be careful to obey all the law My servant Moses gave to you; do not turn from it to the right or to the left, that you may be successful wherever you go (Joshua 1:5–7).

may often question if their activities have value and worth—if they as a person have value and worth. Being is a matter of character. It is a spiritual quality. It is very much a human quality. After all, we are human *beings,* not human *doings.*

In an increasingly fast-paced world, adults must understand their "beingness" so they can help young people come to grips with this concept in their lives. As young people prepare for a career and life in the adult world, the church must provide opportunities for them to explore ways they can define their *being.*

Use the Word of God for this exploration. God—the Supreme Being, Creator of the universe, Giver of life and salvation through Jesus Christ—cares first of all about our *being.* He has proven this—He has completed the act of salvation. Jesus did it on the cross. We don't have to do anything. God did this so that we could be with Him for eternity. If our *being* is in Christ Jesus, then what we *do* will reflect that relationship we have with God and will exhibit love and a sense of trust in Him that will guide our ways.

In Joshua 1, we find a young Joshua who has just started a new job. Moses has recently died and Joshua was now given the responsibility of leading the Israelites into the Promised Land. God speaks a few words to Joshua as he takes on this new position. (In our modern-day world, someone who starts a new job often gets advice on what to do in that new position.) God does not tell Joshua what to do; He tells him how to *be.* He says, "*Be* strong and courageous." These are words of character. God knew that whatever Joshua had to decide as he led Israel, a strong and courageous character would help him perform well. God also gave Joshua a sense of hope and confidence that he could confide in Him. He said, "I will *be* with you; I will never leave you or forsake you." What words of comfort! What words of strength! They are a source of power that Joshua could go to in time of trouble.

God offers that same source of comfort and strength for us today. He will be with us in all of our confusion about life. He will be with young people as they try to decide what they want to do for a career. The promise he made Joshua—"I will never leave you or forsake you"—is a promise that He continues to make to us each and every day.

Prayer

Gracious God, Supreme Being of the universe, You are indeed all-knowing, all-seeing, and almighty. Thank You for Your gracious love expressed in the suffering, death, and resurrection of Your Son, Jesus Christ. Help me to be strong and courageous in the face of the many decisions I make every day. Help me to use my time wisely, and to make good choices in all I do. Strengthen my relationship with You, so that Your love may be reflected in me. In Jesus' name. Amen.

For Further Study

Our loving God desires that we enjoy His gift of life here on earth. Listed below are several passages of Scripture that tell about the kind of life that God has planned for His people.

1 Peter 2:4–10—God has a special plan for His people through Jesus Christ.

1 Cor. 12:12–27—Paul writes of the place that we all have in the work of the Kingdom.

Ex. 3–4—God gives Moses a new job and His promise of being with him as he undertakes new responsibilities.

For Reflection

1. How much time do you spend on **doing?** What are some **doings** in your life that you could give up?
2. Why does our society focus so much on **doing?** How can this be harmful?
3. What elements of being would you like to develop in your life? How might you go about developing those character elements?
4. How can you develop a better balance between your doing and being?

See Power Plays, Book 2, Study 5—

"How Will I Know When I've Got It Made?"

The Honor Roll

"S-U-C-C-E-S-S—that's the way you spell success!" So goes the familiar cheer. Spelling success is easy. Achieving it is harder. Measuring whether or not you have achieved it is harder still.

The real problem is defining success. Is it a goal, or is it a process? Is it something you do? Is it something you are? Does success mean the same thing to all people?

The dictionary defines success as "turning out as hoped." If that definition is true, success would depend on what you hope for. Human beings hope for many things—wealth, fame, a loving family, meaningful work. And just as the dictionary suggests, we judge ourselves as successes—or failures—according to these goals.

Sometimes hopes are unrealistic, like a 5-foot, 2-inch athlete who feels like a failure when he doesn't make the basketball team. Sometimes hopes seem realistic but are never achieved, like the attractive, outgoing person who never marries. Sometimes the goal, when achieved, doesn't seem so satisfying after all. A person may look like a success, but not feel like one. She may have lots of money, but constantly worries about getting more. He may have a challenging job, but still feels driven to push for a promotion. She may have a faithful husband and family, yet wonder what it would be like to have chosen a different path. Have they succeeded or failed?

Achieving our own goals can be difficult enough. More pressure can come from others telling us what we should or shouldn't

Bible Text

The seventy-two returned with joy and said, "Lord, even the demons submit to us in Your name." He replied, "I saw Satan fall like lightening from heaven. I have given you authority to ... overcome all the power of the enemy; nothing will harm you. However, do not rejoice that the spirits submit to you, but rejoice that your names are written in heaven" **(Luke 10:17–20).**

> **W**hen what we hope for is what God hopes for us, that we spend eternity with Him, we are assured of success.

achieve. If you don't have a "My child was Student of the Month" sticker on your bumper, are you still a successful parent? If the Perma-Prest isn't, and your husband goes to work in a wrinkled shirt, are you still a successful wife? If your car isn't as new as the Jones', and there's never enough money in your bank account, are you still a successful provider? If the attendance is low and the offering is meager, are you still a successful church worker?

And what if what you had hoped for or what others have achieved never happens to you? What if you never make the honor roll or win a prize or bring home a trophy? Can you still be a success as a person?

God's Word has Good News for us. Yes! We can!

First, Jesus puts our goals in perspective. In Luke 10:17–20, we see 72 of His disciples returning after an exciting foray. Their hopes had been realized. They had labored like lambs among wolves. They had toiled in the harvest fields. They had healed the sick and preached the Gospel throughout the land. They had survived rejection and were full of joy and excitement, heady with success, as they reported their achievements. "We even cast out demons in Your name!" they exclaimed.

"Casting out demons is pretty impressive, all right" is the spirit of Jesus' reply. "But, don't think *that* makes you successful. What should really delight you is that your names are written in heaven."

Here is a hope that can be accomplished; here is a hope that *has been* accomplished. As Paul puts it, "This is a trustworthy saying that deserves full acceptance (and for this we labor and strive), that we have put our hope in the living God, who is the Savior of all men" (1 Tim. 4:9–10). He goes on, "Command those who are rich in this present world not to be arrogant nor to put their hope in wealth, which is so uncertain, but to put their hope in God, who richly provides us with everything for our enjoyment" (1 Tim. 6:17).

> To succeed in this life, as God's redeemed children, means following Jesus.

When what we hope for is what God hopes for us, that we spend eternity with Him, we are assured of success. Paul reminds us that our faith rests "on the hope of eternal life, which God, who does not lie, promised before the beginning of time" (Titus 1:2).

From the beginning of time, God's bumper sticker has proclaimed, "My child is on the honor roll of heaven." We have been measured according to God's grace and have been declared "success-*full*." Our empty lives have been filled by the power of the Holy Spirit with all the components that success entails.

For Further Study

The Old Testament is rich with passages that refer to success or succeeding. In nearly every case success is measured according to what is God's will, not according to the expectations of people.

You might wish to explore the following:

Gen. 24—Abraham's servant searches for a wife for Isaac.

Gen. 39–41—Joseph rises to power in Egypt.

Num. 13–14—Israel has "second thoughts" about entering Canaan from the south.

Neh. 1–2—Nehemiah works to rebuild Jerusalem's wall.

Prov. 16:3 and 21:30—Solomon gives advice.

Dan. 11—Daniel has a vision of plans that will not succeed.

For Reflection

1. Have you ever won a prize or trophy? How did you feel? Have you ever failed to win a prize or trophy? Does it bother you? Why or why not?

2. Name two people you consider to be successful. Tell why. What characteristics of these people do you see in yourself?

3. In what ways was Jesus a success when He lived on this earth? In what ways would He be considered a failure?

4. Think of some specific people you know—family members, co-workers, those you teach or serve. Are they feeling successful or tasting failure? How can you help them experience the joy of success through Christ?

- *Fame?* We are known intimately by the almighty God.
- *Fortune?* Our treasure is incorruptible, stored up for us in heaven, a free gift from the limitless resources of our heavenly Father.
- *Power?* We can do all things through Christ, who strengthens us.
- *Prestige?* We are the children of the King of kings.

Since we have been found to be successful, we have nothing left but to succeed. To succeed, again according to the dictionary is to "follow, as in office; to come after."

"If anyone would come after Me," says Jesus, "he must deny himself and take up his cross and follow Me. For whoever wants to save his life will lose it, but whoever loses his life for Me will find it" (Matt. 16:24–25).

To succeed in this life, as God's redeemed children, means following Jesus. Success in the eyes of Jesus may not look like success in the eyes of the world. It may not feel like success to you. But in God's way of looking at things, you have turned out exactly as He had hoped. Rejoice. By the grace of God, You are on His honor roll for all eternity.

That is the way you spell success!

Prayer

Thank God for the material successes He has allowed you to experience.

Pray for forgiveness for the feelings of pride that accompanied your successes.

Pray for encouragement when you feel you are a failure.

Pray for encouragement for others who are feeling unsuccessful.

Thank God for the certainty of spending eternity with Him in heaven.

See Power Plays, Book 2, Study 6—

"Special People, Special Purpose"

In Sexuality—a Pig or a Bride?

To the pig, being up to your snout in mud and manure is not all that bad. In fact, it's pretty warm and cozy. If you've ever watched one, you know that the pig will go out of its way to burrow in muck. When offered a clean stall or a mud hole, the pig will choose the mud.

In marked contrast to the pig is the bride on her wedding day. After hours of preparation, primping, and dressing she looks more like a fashion doll than a living person. Adorned with jewels and a shimmering white dress and veil, she is the picture of perfection as she awaits her groom. She takes the utmost care in her walk and her expressions as she fills the bridal role. This is *her* moment. Imagine the bride stepping out of her dressing room and falling in up to her neck in manure. To say the least, she would be horrified.

Why then is the bride of Christ content to wallow in muck when it comes to our human sexuality? The statistics for "churched" or "Christian" teens are not much different from nonbelievers when it comes to sexual activity. Why is it that we seem to be failing in the area of sexual purity?

Perhaps it is because we have been fed the lie that our identity as God's chosen, holy nation can be separated from our sexuality. Perhaps it is because, as we look around us, there are so many other people in the mud and manure that it doesn't seem so bad. In fact, it looks pretty warm and cozy.

> We find our hope, joy, and purpose in our identity as His children.

Bible Text

Therefore, since we are surrounded by such a great cloud of witnesses, let us throw off everything that hinders and the sin that so easily entangles, and let us run with perseverance the race marked out for us. Let us fix our eyes on Jesus, the author and perfecter of our faith, who for the joy set before Him endured the cross, scorning its shame, and sat down at the right hand of the throne of God. Consider Him who endured such opposition from sinful men, so that you will not grow weary and lose heart (Hebrews 12:1–3).

For Further Study

"Fixing our eyes on Jesus" involves studying His Word and understanding who He made us to be. A great way to begin that process is to memorize and apply Scripture in our lives. Here are a few to get you started:

1 John 3:1—We are called "children of God."

2 Cor. 5:17—We are a new creation in Christ.

Is. 43:1—God has called us by name.

1 Peter 2:9–10—We are a royal priesthood.

John 15:15–16—We are chosen by Christ.

Rom. 8:1–2—There is now no condemnation in Christ.

Our world is full of pigs in mud. They seem to go out of their way to insist that everyone who is not burrowing in muck is out of touch and wrong. The world around us appears determined to drag us down into the manure.

The world hasn't changed much since the book of Hebrews was written. God's people in those times faced many temptations and distractions that would pull them away from their holy identity as His beloved. They too struggled with hindrances and entanglements. They too were constantly pressured to leave the race that was marked out for them. In the midst of this struggle, the author of Hebrews offers us a key in remaining faithful to the path laid out for us.

Where does one receive the power to keep from wallowing in the mire and instead to run with perseverance? "Fix your eyes on Jesus." Our problem with sexuality is not so much solved by suppressing hormones as it is by reclaiming our identity. We have forgotten who we really are. We have lost sight of our image, as the bride of Christ, and our eyes are drawn to the deceptive smiles and apparent satisfaction of the pigs in muck. After a while, we forget the white robe and jeweled crown with which we have been adorned (Rev. 7:13–14; 3:11). "That mud doesn't look too terribly bad and, hey, the pigs look like they're having a good time," we muse, and in no time at all we find ourselves longing to join in.

In the middle of this kind of thinking the writer of Hebrews shouts, "Get your eyes back on Jesus!" Consider this Jesus, the One who redeemed you, the One who gave His life for you, the One who has robed you in white and placed a jeweled crown on your head.

> ... through God's cleansing and sustaining power we may live unstained even in a world of muck and pigs.

Remember who and *whose* you are. Remember what He has done for you. Jesus endured the cross, scorning its shame, that we might be set free. Because of Jesus' faithfulness to the path God had set out for Him, He now sits at the right hand of God. Our place, as His chosen and beloved, is with Him in glory, not in the slimy pit. In this world, where pigs in muck may be the norm, our Savior has won for us a high and holy position. We find our hope, joy, and purpose in our identity as His children. We understand that compromising our sexuality means losing sight of that identity. We receive the power to channel our sexuality in God-pleasing ways.

Our identity is established by the robe, the crown, and our home. Our sexuality is a gift with which God has blessed us as His people, His bride. Our sexuality is simply one part of that white robed identity. As the mud flies around us, we hear the constant message, to us, "Jump in!" and it is nearly impossible to keep that gift unstained and used as God intended. Our human condition, the sin and temptation with which we still struggle, may cause us to fall in, to give in. We may take this great and holy gift and find ourselves in a stained robe and muddied crown. One practical suggestion which often does not occur to young people is to avoid places and situations where passion can overcome Christian purpose. Intentionally being alone in private with a person to whom one is sexually attracted will inevitably result in temptation and weakened self-control. We lose sight of our identity and find ourselves with the pigs.

The answer is the same: "Fix your eyes on Jesus." His blood, shed on the cross is a cleansing tide, a forgiving and purifying free-flowing sacrifice that alone washes our robe to the brightest white and sets the sparkle back in our crown, that empowers us to leave the muck and follow Jesus. The gift is made new again; our identity has been reestablished; we are the spotless bride of Christ, once again prepared for the wedding day.

Our text from Hebrews gives us great hope—hope that through God's cleansing and sustaining power we may live unstained even in a world of muck and pigs.

Prayer

Reflect for a few minutes on your sexuality. Take some time to

- thank God for your identity in Christ;
- confess those things that have or might make you lose sight of that identity;
- rejoice that in Christ we are made new each day to live as His chosen brides.

For Reflection

1. Why is sexual temptation so attractive and so difficult to avoid?

2. How can a strong identity of who we are in God's eyes help us determine sexual guidelines that honor God? How can it help us follow these guidelines?

3. What are some ways we, as Christians, can encourage each other and those we teach or serve to live according to our identity as God's spotless bride?

See Power Plays Book 2, Study 7—
"Who Values Life?"

The Value of a Life

On February 3, 1994, at The National Prayer Breakfast in Washington, D.C. with 3,000 of our country's leaders including the President and Vice President, Mother Theresa shared these thoughts:

> And if we accept that a mother can kill even her own child, how can we tell other people not to kill one another? How do we persuade a woman not to have an abortion? As always, we must persuade her with love as we remind ourselves that love means to be willing to give until it hurts. Jesus gave even His life to love us. So the mother who is thinking of abortion should be helped to love, that is, to give until it hurts her plans or her free time, to respect the life of her child.

Incredibly tough words come from such a gentle-spirited woman. But the force of these words bring us face to face with a critical issue in our times: the sanctity of life. According to *Webster's Dictionary*, sanctity is "the state of being consecrated to a deity." In Christian terms, calling something sanctified means that it is special to God Himself. God claims ownership over all life (Ps. 24:1, Ezek. 18:4, Acts 17:25–26). Mankind is created in the very image of God (Gen. 2:7). Our lives are precious to God because they are a reflection of that image. That is why God sets up such strict standards concerning how we treat human life (Gen. 9:6, Ex. 20:13, Matt. 5:21–22).

Yet consider the complexities in this life God has given us. The victim of a head injury can be "brain dead" but physically alive. A 35-year-old victim of Lou Gehrig's disease may no longer want to live. A child in the womb can be diagnosed with Tay-sachs disease which condemns her to a brief, suffering existence. Suddenly the arguments concerning "quality of life" begin to come into

Bible Text

For You created my inmost being; You knit me together in my mother's womb. I praise You because I am fearfully and wonderfully made; Your works are wonderful, I know that full well. My frame was not hidden from You when I was made in the secret place. When I was woven together in the depths of the earth, Your eyes saw my unformed body. All the days ordained for me were written in Your book before one of them came to be
(Psalm 139:13–16).

> It is God who determines the value of life because it is God who knits value into it.

play. Currently, the debate swirls around who has the right to decide whether someone should live or die. The controversy encompasses such issues as abortion, euthanasia, and biomedical ethics.

The words of Psalm 139 lift the issue of the sanctity of life above politics, special agendas, and personal rights. Psalm 139 returns life to the hand from which it came—God's. God is pictured as a weaver, absorbed in a miraculous creation. With each strand, heavenly hands infuse a little more of the image of the Creator into the creation. And as the weaver keeps in mind the image of the completed whole, so our Father sees each day that has been laid out for us long before the weaving is complete.

Life is sacred because it is inseparably connected to the Creator. It is God who determines the value of life because it is God who knits value into it. The quality of life does not have as much to do with ease and comfort of living as it does with a close relationship to the One who gives life.

Mother Theresa exposed one central truth—sometimes life hurts. Becoming pregnant from rape, watching over a comatose loved one on life support, caring for a cancer patient who continually begs to die rather than slowly die an excruciating death—these are terrible hurts. The answer is not to take life out of the hands of the Creator and settle it according to the judgments of the creature. The answer is, in Mother Theresa's words, to "give until it hurts."

Jesus is our Priest and King because He gave His life on the cross. There is no hurt we can experience that He does not personally know. On the cross we see Jesus bearing the pain of the violated, frightened unwed mother, the cancer victim in agony, the family of the patient on life support. He did not die so that we could narrowly define the value of life, but that we may live life to the fullest in whatever the circumstances.

Martin Luther shares this in his explanation of the Fifth Commandment: "We should fear and love God so that we do not hurt or harm our neighbor in his body, but help and support him in every physical need."

The best way to sanctify life is for us to "give until it hurts." Each life has value because it is created by the hand of God in the image of God. In order to persuade others that each life is sacred, we—like the woman considering abortion—must love until it hurts our plans or free time, until we have loved like Christ. Through the love of Christ in us, others will truly know that life itself is holy. It has infinite value because it is God Himself who gives it.

Prayer

Take a moment to read the words from Psalm 139. Imagine God's hands as He "knit" you together in your mother's womb. Spend time thanking Him for yourself, a fearfully and wonderfully made life. Then ask Him to give you opportunity to share with someone who is hurting the healing, life-valuing love of Christ.

For Further Study

Life issues are tough, especially when it comes to "pulling the plug" and other complex decisions. As life is a gift of God, so is His grace, His presence in each and everyone of these tough situations. The following verses can encourage us to ask for and follow His guidance as we seek to hold life holy unto Him.

Is. 42:16—God is our guide.

Ps. 62:5–8—God is our rock and salvation.

Deut. 32:39—Life is in God's hand.

Acts 17:24–28—In Him life has meaning.

For Reflection

1. There is enough pain in our lives without looking for other people's. But trying to feel what others are feeling can show us how to help them. List some of the feelings of the various people in the situations previously mentioned.

2. Pick one of the situations. What "hurts" might you personally have to experience to show them the love of Christ?

3. What kinds of things could the church, the body of Christ, do to help people understand and accept God's view of the sanctity of life?

See Power Plays, Book 2, Study 8—"God Created Sex!"

Positive Sexuality

We live in a sex-saturated society. Sex appeal is used to sell everything from soup to sports stars. We are led to believe that everybody is having lots of sex, and that there is something wrong with those who aren't. Sexual intercourse, we are led to believe, is the logical conclusion of an evening of social interaction between two people even if they just met! It's natural! Exciting! Glamorous!

Studies show this attitude is prevalent among young people as well as adults. According to the definitive survey, *Sex in America,* "half the teenagers of various racial and ethnic groups in the nation have begun having intercourse with a partner in the age range of 15–18, and at least four out of five have had intercourse by the time their teenage years are over" (Robert T. Michal, John H. Gagnon, Edward O. Laumann, and Gina Kolata, *Sex in America,* Little, Brown and Co., Boston, 1994, pp. 91–92). Though the government has spent millions of dollars handing out condoms and providing "safe sex" education to children, the facts are that these programs have failed miserably. Sexual intercourse and pregnancies among unmarried teens continue to rise. One out of three babies is born out of wedlock in the United States.

Christian parents want to know "How to Raise Sexually Pure Kids in an 'Anything Goes' World" (the subtitle of a book by Tim and Beverly LaHaye). Young people want to know "how far is too far." Education that was once the responsibility of family and church has shifted to government and schools. Years ago the church was the conscience of the majority of the people. Today, government, television, the media, and our schools have become the "new" conscience. If a correct understanding of sexu-

Bible Text

Flee from sexual immorality. All other sins a man commits are outside his body, but he who sins sexually sins against his own body. Do you not know that your body is a temple of the Holy Spirit, who is in you, whom you have received from God? You are not your own; you were bought at a price. Therefore honor God with your body **(1 Corinthians 6:18–20).**

His Word teaches us that sexuality is God's creation, His plan, His gift to us.

ality and its use is to be regained, it must come from those who acknowledge the authority of God's Word. His Word teaches us that sexuality is God's creation, His plan, His gift to us. God instructs us on how to use this gift in many different Scriptural passages including 1 Cor. 6:18–20.

The media these days is quick to shine the public spotlight on allegations of sexual misconduct among Christian leaders. It should not surprise us that Christian adults, including those who serve in leadership or teaching positions in the church, may struggle with sin in this area as in all others. They—and we—are not immune to the devil's temptations to sin. God would have us flee from them, however, and offers us His power to do so.

Through this passage by St. Paul, God makes it clear that we belong to Him, not just our souls, but our bodies as well. God redeemed us from sin, death, and the power of the devil with Jesus' life, suffering, death, and resurrection. The analogy of being "bought at a price" comes from a custom during Paul's time. Earthly slaves could pay a price for liberty into a god's temple, and thus become the god's property and free from their earthly masters. If He had not bought us back, we would have been forever enslaved. He has not only purchased us, but set up residency in us. We have become His temple wherein the Holy Spirit dwells. Thus, we are not our own, but His own (John 13:1).

God tells us to "flee from sexual immorality" such as fornication and adultery because it causes us to deny the union we have with Christ. It is what David should have done when he saw Bathsheba on the roof bathing (2 Sam. 11:2ff.). Our power to make a fast exodus away from these sexual sins comes from the Holy Spirit living in us. "Therefore honor God with your body" (1 Cor. 6:20). By the Spirit's power, we display the Lord Jesus Christ who purchased us and dwells within us through the Holy Spirit. The God who did not spare His only begotten Son, Jesus Christ, to die for us also gives us everything else we need (Rom. 8:32).

Prayer

Spend a few minutes in prayer

- to thank God for your own gift of sexuality;
- to ask forgiveness for not always giving honor to God in the way you have used this gift;
- to thank Him for the forgiveness He gives you for all sins you commit, including the sin of misusing the gift of sexuality;
- to ask for guidance and help in teaching others what God, the Creator, says about this gift.

For Further Study

In order to speak confidently and with authority about sexuality we ourselves must know what the Creator of sexuality says about it. Study the following:

Gen. 1:26–27; 2:24; 3:7–22—Sexuality is God's creation.

Prov. 5:18–20; 1 Cor. 7:3–5; Song of Sol. 5:3; 10–16; 8:6—Physical love is for pleasure.

1 Cor. 7:2—Physical love is reserved for a marriage relationship.

Mal. 4:6—Sexual attitudes of parents are transferred to children.

For Reflection

1. God's Word, specifically the Sixth Commandment, teaches abstinence from sexual intercourse until marriage. This is a negative message with a very positive intent. Does your church teach this Word from God clearly?

2. Is the message your church teaches about sexuality only negative? If so, how might sexualy be taught in a more positive way?

3. How could your church teach not only the youth but also the entire congregation what God says about sexuality?

See Power Plays, Book 2, Study 9—
"Me First?"

When Is Enough?

Do you ever feel like your life is one continual give? Everyone makes demands on your time. Your family needs you, those you work with need you, your friends require time and attention.

In a typical day you probably rise early, work through lunch, attend to errands after work, do volunteer work or socialize in the evening, and get phone calls late into the night. You have little discretionary time. You have a lot to do. You are busy. You are tired.

Jesus knows your exhaustion and frustration. He came as a man to experience humanity fully.

Take a look at a day in the life of Jesus as described in the book of Mark. Mark wastes no time getting into the heart of Jesus' ministry. No sweet Christmas story eases us into Mark's gospel. Jesus from the start is full-grown and about His business. Mark sets the stage with John the Baptist, who immediately introduces us to Jesus. Already in the first half of chapter 1 we see Jesus *coming* out of the baptismal waters, *being tempted* in the desert, and *calling* disciples. He *acts*.

The day on which Mark focuses begins (v. 21) with Jesus teaching in the synagog. He amazes people with His authority. He sternly casts a demon out of a member of the congregation. Then He goes home with Peter for the day and heals Peter's mother-in-law just in time for dinner. In the evening, He tries to rest after an exhausting day. But clamoring at Peter's door stands the entire town—everyone with needs and desires and requests for Jesus' help. You can imagine Him far into the night counseling, healing, driving out

Bible Text

Let us not become weary in doing good, for at the proper time we will reap a harvest if we do not give up **(Galatians 6:9).**

> People today have the same needs. They come looking for Jesus. And they may seek Him in you.

demons—just one more time. All this happened on the Sabbath—a day of rest!

The next day the pattern repeats. Jesus rises early, before dawn, and finds a quiet place for solitude, prayer, and renewal. But people in need seek Him out. "Jesus," Peter reports, "everyone is looking for You!"

Instead of burrowing deeper into seclusion, Jesus moves on. "Let's get *going!*" He directs. "There are more places to go, people to see, things to do. That is why I have come."

And He did. He kept going, and going, and going until He could no longer go anywhere without a commotion. Even when He tried to avoid the limelight, Mark says in the last verse of this action-packed chapter, "Yet the people still came to Him from everywhere." They came because He had what they needed—help, healing of body and mind, the forgiveness of sins.

Jesus knew exhaustion and frustration. Yet He had sources of strength in the midst of it all to carry on—sources of strength which we can find as well. He was one with God the Father. We cannot share His divinity, but we can find strength in our relationship with God our Father. God loves us and promises us strength to accomplish all that He requires.

Jesus kept His priorities straight. In Mark 1, and throughout the Gospels, we see Jesus finding strength through devotional time spent in prayer. Like Jesus, and with His help, we can make such devotional time a priority. Personal Bible study, meditation, prayer, and recreation are important components in a balanced life of service.

Jesus trusted in His Father's will (Mark 14:36). We can be confident in God's ability to accomplish His will. We are not alone in our tasks of service; we are not His only tools. Our desire to serve should not be a blasphemous anxiety that seeks to take responsibility for a work load only God can handle. Remember that Paul admitted, "I planted the seed, Apollos watered it, but God made it grow" (1 Cor. 3:6).

People today have the same needs. They come looking for Jesus. And they may seek Him in you.

> God has already supplied you with enough resources to succeed—His forgiving love, His power, His Spirit.

For Further Study

Are there times when you may think that your spiritual "well" has run dry and you have no resources left from which to draw? Reflect on these passages:

2 Cor. 3:3—You are a letter from Christ.

Rom. 15:1–3—In Christ we find strength to help others.

1 Cor. 15:58—You do not work for the Lord in vain.

2 Cor. 6:4–10—Through the power of the Holy Spirit we may endure much hardship, yet we possess everything in Christ.

Look for a copy of **The Contemplative Pastor** (Eugene Peterson, Eerdmans, 1993); it has an excellent section on building up our relationship with God.

For Reflection

1. List three things about your work in the church that give you joy. Share them with someone.

2. If you are a professional church worker, why did you become one? Do you feel people are aware of all your responsibilities or appreciate all your efforts? Why are you **still** a worker in the church?

3. If you are not a professional church worker, do you find it easy or difficult to serve other people, to volunteer for extra duties?

4. What "demon" in your own life continually brings you to Jesus for casting out? What "demons" do you see plaguing people who come to you?

They may find you teaching a Bible class, or kicking off your shoes at the end of the day, or trying to get away for a little peace and quiet. They seek you out because their demons are real, and they can't wait. You know what demons are. They have names like drugs and abuse, self-doubt and guilt, confusion and pain.

You and I are blessed to be a part of God's harvest. We have been forgiven and brought into God's kingdom. Our demons have been dealt with. We have been touched by Jesus' healing hand. Now we are privileged to *be* His hands in the harvest field in which we live.

We can share the joy that comes from giving ourselves for others in response to Jesus' love for us. By the power of the Holy Spirit, we can encourage future workers in the harvest field. We can show them, give them opportunities, teach them how to carry on the never-ending task.

In our efforts to "do it all" we frequently attempt too much. Our exhaustion stems not from too little time, but failure to invest our time wisely. God in His grace empowers us in our relationship with Him, nurtured through Bible study and devotional time, to make wise choices in the activities with which we fill our time. With His help we can be effective workers in the harvest, free from undue exhaustion or frusration and full of joy.

Prayer

Thank God for making You His co-laborer in bringing in His harvest.
Pray for energy and endurance in times of weariness.
Pray for the needs of specific people who are in your care.
Ask God to move young people to be willing to give of themselves in the service of others.

Music and Its Influence

See Power Plays, Book 2, Study 10—
"My Music—To God's Glory!"

Next to theology, I give to music the highest place and the greatest honor. I would not exchange what little I know of music for something great. ... My heart bubbles up and overflows in response to music, which has so often refreshed me and delivered me from dire plagues.

Martin Luther speaks of the beauty and honor of music. Luther also used music to ease his burdens. Today, music sometimes *places* heavy burdens on its singers and listeners. Many parents say that the music their children listen to is ruining their lives. But it certainly doesn't have to be this way, especially for the Christian listener and musician.

Bible Text
Rejoice in the Lord always. I will say it again: Rejoice! Let your gentleness be evident to all. The Lord is near. ... Whatever is true, whatever is noble, whatever is right, whatever is pure, whatever is lovely, whatever is admirable—if anything is excellent or praiseworthy—think about such things" **(Philippians 4:4–5, 8).**

Scripture extols the making of music. Sin, however, has tarnished this beautiful gift God gives to people. As we have become disconnected from God because of sin, we also have become disconnected from each other. Much of today's music reflects this disconnection. For example, country music once proclaimed a message of skies that "are not cloudy all day." Now we hear lyrics that tell about people cheating on their spouses, alcohol abuse, aborting babies, and killing one another. Popular music once extolled the joy of "Surfin' USA." Now Guns 'N' Roses sings of taking cocaine and committing murder. The names of some musical groups tell you something about their music. Groups like Snoop Doggy Dogg, Nine Inch Nails, Soul Asylum, Belly, and Sex Pistols speak in their music of stabbings, decapitations, drugs, sex, alcohol, suicide, and the advantages of being bi-sexual.

> Scripture extols the making of music. Sin, however, has tarnished this beautiful gift God gives to people.

For Further Study

Study two New Testament passages which speak of music: Eph. 5:19; Col. 3:16. What do these verses command believers to do? Study the roots of the words *psalms* and *hymns*.

Read and study the great hymns of faith that are found in your hymnal. Such study may yield a new perspective not gained by singing the hymn in worship.

Surveys show that fewer than 10% of Christians listen to Christian music outside the worship service each Sunday morning. Spend some time this week listening to some Christian music. Listen critically, testing the songs against the truth in God's Word. As you discover contemporary songs and songwriters who excel in illuminating the Word, make note of that and share with others.

Study the songs of praise that accompanied the triumphs of God's people: Neh. 12:27–31; 38–43; Num. 21:16–18; and Judges 5. What are your favorite songs of praise and thanksgiving today? Why?

Some argue that none of this music hurts anyone. They propose that the music may contain words that are distasteful but they don't cause people to kill policemen or decapitate someone. Yet we know music—its lyrics and arrangements—*does* impact people. It educates and influences them. It desensitizes them. It evokes emotional and physical responses in our sinful human nature. Through repetition, music's messages—positive or negative—can easily become part of our lives.

We've all heard the expression, "You are what you eat." The same is true when it comes a person's mind and soul. Much of our music today concentrates on that which is dishonorable, displeasing to the Lord. Hence, there is little real joy and peace in many people's lives. Sin breeds sin. Anger breeds anger. Musicians can influence people to accept their messages and mimic the messengers themselves.

In His First Commandment, the Lord commands us to put Him first in our lives, loving Him more than anyone or anything else. His Second Commandment would have us praise His holy name rather than defame and blaspheme Him. God warns us in His Law against despising His Word, dishonoring our parents and others in authority, hurting and killing others, and committing adultery. Through the Spirit living and working in us, we can discern music that is true, right, pure, lovely, and praiseworthy. The Holy Spirit enables us to choose wisely the music we listen to and share with others, that through our actions we might always glorify God.

> Musicians can influence people to accept their messages and mimic the messengers themselves.

The apostle Paul reminded the early Christian community to "rejoice in the Lord" (Phil. 4:4) as he wrote from prison, there because he had spoken of Christ and His atoning sacrifice. The secret to Paul's rejoicing was that he was "in the Lord." He knew that the Christ who had died for him would also provide him with all of his needs (Rom. 8:32). The presence of the Lord in Paul's life was evident in the gentleness he demonstrated to others (Phil. 4:5). Rather than show anger and bitter frustration about his imprisonment, Paul witnessed to his faith and proclaimed Christ. He found opportunities to address the hurts of those who imprisoned him and shared Christ's love with them. Likewise, the presence of the Lord in our lives turns us to think on those things that are "true, noble, right, pure, lovely, admirable, excellent, praiseworthy."

God's desire is for His people to rejoice in life—new life through Jesus Christ. His plan is for every person to know that life in Him does not consist of fears, worries, and earthly concerns; rather, the Christian lives in the hope of eternal life with God and in a life more abundant here on earth (see John 10:10). As both listeners and music-makers, we can live each day as the sanctified people God's Holy Spirit empowers us to be. We can praise, thank, and glorify the Lord through music.

Prayer

Spend a few minutes in prayer using the acronym **A C T S** as a guide.

Adoration—Give adoration to God to that which is "true ... noble ... right ... pure ... lovely ... admirable ... excellent ... praiseworthy" (Phil. 4:8).

Confession—Confess your sin of listening to music that has negatively influenced you.

Thanksgiving—Give thanks to God for the gift of music. Thank Him for Christian hymnwriters, songbooks, and musical artists today.

Supplication—Pray for your children and all young people that they might have God's help in their choices of music and not be led astray by sinful music of any kind.

For Reflection

1. How did Paul and Silas occupy themselves while in prison? (See Acts 16:25.)

2. Think of a time when some outside force or circumstance kept you from rejoicing "in the Lord." What happened that helped you to begin rejoicing again? Offer a prayer of thanksgiving. (If possible, say this prayer with a partner. Or, sing your prayer to your own melody.)

See Power Plays, Book 2, Study 11—

"Whom Do You Admire Most and Why?"

Heroes

It was June 12, 1994. The weather was picture-perfect in Los Angeles, temperature in the mid-70s, with a gentle breeze off the Pacific. However, the pristine day would soon be shattered by two murders. The accused murderer would be O. J. Simpson, sports legend and football star. The news media referred to the fall of O. J. Simpson as a great American tragedy. People spoke of the fall of a great American hero.

Though O. J. Simpson was the recipient of the much-coveted Heisman trophy in 1968, though he broke the all-time, single-season rushing record with 2,003 yards, though he was ushered into the pro football Hall of Fame, though he did commercial endorsements on television, starred in Hollywood movies, and was a successful sportscaster for many years, was he really a hero?

One definition of a hero according to *The American Heritage Dictionary* is "someone who is noted for feats of courage or nobility of purpose; especially, one who has risked or sacrificed his life." According to the definition, even if one puts aside the murder charges, could O. J. Simpson really be thought of as a hero?

The definition, or at least the catalog, of our heroes seems to have changed somewhat over the years. They are rarely the statesmen, soldiers, and benefactors in the world—F. D. Roosevelt, George Patton, Florence Nightingale. They are not even the fictional crusaders of years past—the Lone Ranger, Superman, or Sherlock Holmes.

In reality, our world has spent the last few decades seeking out and admiring celebrities rather than heroes. The characteristics for which many today are "celebrated" has nothing to do with heroism. Many of them are the entertainers in our world—ball players

Bible Text

Worthy is the Lamb, who was slain, to receive power and wealth and wisdom and strength and honor and glory and praise!
(Rev. 5:12).

> A hero—"someone who is noted for feats of courage or nobility of purpose; especially, one who has risked or sacrificed his life."

and sports pros of all kinds, classical and nonclassical musicians, movie and television stars. They are frequently wealthy and often non-conformists. They entertain us with their talents "on stage" and with every detail of their lives "behind the curtain."

Too often, those things for which our celebrities are known show little "nobility of purpose" or "sacrifice." They are not the stuff of heroes.

The truth is, O. J. Simpson is no more a hero than many of the men and women society elevates to celebrity status. We put them on pedestals and forget they are human beings. We idolize them and are surprised when they fall from their high and lofty positions.

Real heroes are often far different than those society admires. True heroes are hard to identify. They don't always look like heroes. They often don't sound like the heroes we hear about over the radio or television. Real heroes can live next door, even in our homes. A real hero can be the man who changes the oil in your car (he doesn't have even a million dollars). Or the day-care worker (she doesn't even know how to play basketball). Or the mother who works an extra job so her children can go to a Christian school. Or the dad who plays softball with his child immediately after work every day of the week.

Remember that first definition of a hero—"someone who is noted for feats of courage or nobility of purpose; especially, one who has risked or sacrificed his life." There is one real Hero—the Lord Jesus Christ. He went to the cross for sins He never committed. Who had a purpose higher than that of Jesus Christ? He was born in a stable among the animals for one purpose, not to live, but to die so that "whoever believes in Him shall not perish but have eternal life" (John 3:16). He sacrificed Himself for the salvation of mankind. As He lives in the hearts of His people, He empowers them for heroic actions in His service.

Human celebrities and heroes will always disappoint us. Only One will not—Jesus Christ. Instead of looking to secular heroes, we can look to God for help and salvation: "Turn to Me and be saved, all you ends of the earth; for I am God, and there is no other" (Is. 45:22).

Prayer

Spend a few minutes in prayer using the following suggestions:

* Give God thanks and praise for a Savior, who was truly a hero in every sense of the word. Thank Him for your greatest gift— redemption through Jesus Christ.
* Recall some earthly heroes in your life who have meant a great deal to you, such as a special mother and/or father, a school teacher, a brother, and give thanks for these people.
* Pray that you might be a hero to others in the way you love them and minister to them. Pray also that you might share the Hero, Jesus Christ, with them.

For Further Study

Celebrities, society's heroes, are often those who are rich in the things of this world. Review some of God's thoughts on money: 1 Tim. 6:9–10; Luke 12:15; Mark 8:36; Luke 6:46–49.

Choose an Old Testament hero and make a detailed study of his/her life. Use a concordance to look up all the passages that detail the hero's life. As you study the person's life, ask yourself whether or not the person would be considered a hero today. Why or why not?

For Reflection

1. Read Mark 1:1–8. Did John the Baptizer appear to be a hero? Why was he a hero?

2. Read 2 Cor. 4:7–11; 6:4–10; 11:22–28. Underline the words that would identify Paul as a hero. Do the passages encourage or discourage you?

3. What makes a person "great"? Is it wrong to strive for greatness?

4. Study Matt. 18:1–5. The disciples wanted to know which of them would be the greatest in heaven. That's when they learned what Jesus' definition of greatness was. In your own words define **greatness.**

5. Who is the greatest person who ever lived? Why?

See Power Plays, Book 2, Study 12—

"Peace of Mind in Violent Times"

Our Violent God?

A single page of a recent daily newspaper featured the following headlines:

> Minneapolis Man Stabbed in Dispute over Loud Music
> Police Seeking Motive in Chicago Woman's Shooting
> Buena Park Man, 23, Fatally Shot in Anaheim
> Victim Survives Ramming of Golf Club Shaft through Head
> U.S. to Dispose of Napalm

Bible Text
God is our refuge and strength, an ever-present help in trouble **(Psalm 46:1).**

If any one issue paints the picture of our modern age, it must be the overwhelming emphasis on violence. We decry it personally and professionally. We plead with the media to control its obsession with bringing violence into our living rooms. We go to great lengths to protect our children from its influence.

> **God does not cause violence, sin does.**

We are definitely *against* violence! Yet we can chuckle at the irony and appreciate the frustration of the Sunday school teacher who screams at the top of her voice, "Sit down and shut up so I can teach you how to be kind and loving!" We realize our own violent feelings are often very close to the surface.

Violence is a part of life this side of heaven, even for God's people. Consider some biblical "headlines" as well.

> Lucifer Cast into Pit of Hell; Vows Revenge
> Global Flooding: All Mankind Perishes
> "God Told Me to Do It," Abraham Pleads
> Sodom Destroyed with Brimstone; No Survivors
> Plagues Strike Egypt; First-born Die

You get the picture. God does not cause violence, sin does. Sin and violence are not God's will for us. Jesus came to overthrow sin and its violent outbursts in our lives.

Jesus scolded James and John for their violent intentions in Luke 9:54; He called them "Sons of thunder" (Mark 3:17).

And remember Peter in the Garden of Gethsemane? "I'll save You!" he shrieked, flailing his sword through the air and cutting off a combatant's ear (Matt. 26:50–55).

But it was Jesus who was to do the saving. The event would be a violent one. In a bloody and terrifying act He would, for all time, *kill* violence. But He had to do it Himself. He alone could destroy violence without letting it destroy Him in the process.

We cannot rid ourselves of violence. It is part of our very nature. "Out of the heart," we are told in Matt. 15:19, "come evil thoughts, murder, adultery, sexual immorality, theft, false testimony, slander." Our problem with violence is not that it exists. Our problem is that violence seems out of control. We are afraid it might be directed against *us!*

This is where Jesus comes in. He takes the scary headlines, the bombarding video assaults, and the ever-encroaching physical threats to our personal safety and eradicates their power over us. With His cross-shaped shield He guards our very hearts from debilitating fear, for He has fought violence —and won! We, like Peter, can put away our swords and take refuge in the shadow of our Champion.

> By faith, Christ is at work in us, turning us from violence to be more like Him.

Will we be the victim of random violence? Will gangs or car-jackers diminish our freedom? Perhaps. Can violence destroy our lives? For a while. But God does not want us to live in fear. He has freed us to live in faith. He does not promise us a life without trouble; He promises us a *refuge* in the midst of life, and life eternal when we die.

Best of all, He has focused the full force of His wrath on the real enemy—Satan himself. He has pulled us out of Satan's grip with His own strong hand and rendered the enemy helpless. He has shown him no mercy, pulled no punches, made no plea bargain. His violence is directed toward the prince of violence.

Since God has taken care of violence, we are now free to be at peace—with ourselves and with others. By faith, Christ is at work in us, turning us from violence to be more like Him. When we

For Further Study

God's Word is one of His tools for our war against the violence of sin in our lives. Consider these passages as you combat violence:

2 Sam. 22:3—God is our shield from violent people.

Ps. 9:9 (and others)—God is our refuge in all trouble.

Rom. 12:19—God reserves for Himself the role of avenger and judge.

Phil. 4:13—God gives us strength.

Col. 3:13—The Lord's forgiveness empowers us to forgive.

For Reflection

1. What really makes you mad? Do you feel capable of doing something violent to the person who causes you to feel so angry?

2. Identify three violent movies or television programs. What can you do to counteract their effect on you or your family?

3. Think about a time you lost your temper. How did you express your anger? Did you hurt anyone else in the process?

4. Do you think young people in our society are desensitized to the effects of violence? How does it express itself? How can it be counteracted? Give examples to support your opinion.

could insist upon revenge, we can forgive. When people deserve to be punished, we can demonstrate mercy. Instead of expressing hate and bitterness, we can relax in His love. As new creations by the Spirit, we can live differently.

Thank God for taking sin seriously—for reacting violently and unleashing His righteous anger against it, for nothing less than His gracious love could have saved us from its power.

How far would you go to protect the lives of those you love? Would you not fight to your death, if necessary, in order to save them?

That's exactly what Jesus did. He fought to His death to defend the ones He loves the most—you and me. In doing so, He gave us an alternative. "All they who live by the sword shall die by the sword," he warned Peter. Those who live by His cross, however, will never perish, but have everlasting life.

Prayer

Pray for forgiveness for the times you have expressed your anger in hurtful ways.

Pray for people who live by violence; pray for their victims as well.

Pray for protection for yourself and your family in your daily lives.

Pray for courage to live without fear in this world.